Madonna

Biography

Life and Musical Legacy of an Icon

CONTENT

1. Restless Child

2. Confusing Times

3. Losing Her Virginity

4. Busting Out

5. Certain Sacrifices

6. Madonna: The Debut Album

7. The Affair with Prince

8. "Madonna: A Lonely Life"

9. The Remaking of Apocalypse Now

10. Trouble in "Paradise"

11. Who's That Girl?

12. Dinner with Warren

13. Malibu Nightmare

14. Divorce

15. I'm Breathless

16. Warren Proposes Marriage to Madonna?

17. Sex

18. Erotica

19. Bad Career Moves

20. Trash Talking on TV

21. Bedtime Stories

22. Stalked

23. Something to Remember

24. The Stalking Trial

25. A Race to the Finish

26. No Big Thing?

27. Betrayal

28. Role Model?

29. Anticlimax

30. Ray of Light

31. Madonna's Moment

32. Music

33. Happy Endings

1.Restless Child

Who is this person capable of beguiling a country's president into doing something he had no intention of doing, and doing it her way? What is it about this lady — an entertainer who isn't unusually gorgeous and, while brilliant, perhaps not fantastically so — that has kept her at the top of the show business ladder for the last fifteen years as the very symbol of success and glamour? Always at ease and confident within her own limitations, she stated in her 1991 documentary film Truth or Dare, "I know I'm not the best singer or dancer in the world." That I am aware of. But I'm also not interested in that. "I'm fascinated by pushing buttons."

Many journalists have gone back and researched Madonna's past in the years following her initial popularity in 1983, looking for clues to the enigma of Madonna. However, Madonna Louise Veronica Ciccone's modest origins gave little indication of what was to come.

"I get nostalgic for a time in my life before I was an empire," Madonna stated in an online discussion with AOL customers in September 2000. Madonna, like many others who become famous, wanted to be a star before she became "an empire." A burning desire to be renowned appeared to be formed within her, as if it were a fundamental part of who she was. When she finally achieved her dream, one of her most famous quotes was, "I have the same goal I've had since I was a little girl." "I want to be King of the World."

Despite being half French Canadian, Madonna appears to identify primarily with her other half, her Italian origin. When she performed in Italy in the summer of 1987, she told an audience of 65,000 admirers at the Turin football stadium, "Io sono fiera di essere Italiana" ("I'm proud to be an Italian"). Her Italian ancestors came from the Abruzzi province of Pacentro in the 1800s. Nicola Pietro

Ciccone, her paternal great-grandfather, was born in Pacentro in 1867. He married Anna Maria Mancini, also from Pacentro, when he was twenty-six years old. They had a son, Gaetano, Madonna's grandfather, in 1901. Eighteen years later, Gaetano married Michelina (there appears to be no record of her surname), also from the area. Soon after, the couple relocated to the United States, residing in the Pittsburgh suburb of Aliquippa. Gaetano worked in the steel mills of Pittsburgh, despite his inability to communicate in English. They had their first child, Mario, in 1930, and their second son, Silvio — nicknamed Tony — Madonna's father, four years later. Over the next six years, four additional children, all males, would be born.

On May 4, 1956, Madonna Fortin Ciccone gave birth to the couple's first child, Anthony. Martin, another son, was born a year later, on August 9. Madonna Fortin Ciccone gave birth to her first daughter, Madonna Louise (nicknamed "Nonnie" by her parents) in Bay City Mercy Hospital on August 16, 1958, while visiting her mother, Elsie Fortin. Over the next three years, she would give birth to three more children, Paula, Christopher, and Melanie.

"I grew up in a really big family and in an environment where you had to get over it to be heard," Madonna said in a previous interview. "I felt like the devil. It seemed like I was living in a zoo. You had to tell everyone everything. For years, I shared a bed — not even a double bed — with two sisters." She went on to say, "I would even hurt myself, like burn my fingers deliberately, to get attention."

"She was spoiled from the start," her brother Christopher recalls. "She was the oldest girl, and she was our parents' favourite." That, combined with the fact that she was quite pushy and demanded and received her way, made her a spoilt child. But she was a good person. She enjoyed looking after the group. "She was also quite bossy," he adds. "Very bossy."

Growing up, Madonna had always been a die-hard devotee of classic Hollywood and its icons. She realised at a young age that many of the world's biggest entertainers had turbulent early lives filled with mystery and drama. She was a theatrical child who seemed to understand the significance of folklore. Years later, Madonna appeared to want to give the idea that she came from a lower-income family in interviews, maybe wanting to profit on the "good copy" value of the so-called traditional rags-to-riches story. While this appeared to be the kind of background she wanted to claim for herself — one in which she had to overcome huge childhood traumas and barriers before she could even consider achieving success — it wasn't the case.

Silvio, her father, was never unemployed. Even with the responsibility of so many children and the financial weight that comes with having a large family, he fared well. Madonna has always led a healthy, middle-class life.

"Ours was a strict, old-fashioned family," she explained. "When I was a little girl, my grandmother begged me to go to church with her, to love Jesus and to be a good girl." I was raised with two stereotypes of women: the virgin and the whore."

Madonna was extremely close to her mother when she was a child. The two Madonnas had a deep and particular bond, and throughout her career, daughter would always speak fondly of mother. "She was beautiful," Madonna said of her mother, "and very loving and devoted to her children." Very child-centred." Her earliest childhood recollections are cheerful, she claims, because they revolved around her mother, whom she also describes as "forgiving and angelic."

"When I was four and younger, I remember not being able to sleep at night," she recalls. "I'd walk into my parents' bedroom and open the door." They were both asleep in bed, and I believe I must have gone in there frequently because they both rose up in bed and exclaimed,

'Oh no, not again!' 'Can I go to bed with you?' I said. My father was opposed to me sleeping with them. Nonetheless, I recall climbing into bed and rubbing against my mother's really lovely, scarlet, silky nightgown... and falling asleep — just like that. When I was among them, I always fell asleep right away. Even though my siblings and sisters were in my room with me, I felt quite lonely and lonesome. As a result, I desired to sleep with my parents. Sleeping with my parents was nirvana for me."

Martin, Madonna's older brother, recalls her as a restless, hyperactive child. Despite their customary sibling rivalry, little Nonnie never let her older brother intimidate her. If he put Vaseline in her hair while she slept or hung her by her underpants on the clothesline, she'd quickly react by snitching on him the next time he sneaked out of the home and went down to the corner store without permission. Madonna didn't like anyone getting the best of her from a young age, and she resented being told what to do and how to act, even by her parents. "When I was a child, I always thought the world was mine," she remarked, "that it was a playground for me, full of opportunities." "I've always had the attitude that I was going to go out into the world and do whatever I wanted to do."

No child likes being told what to do, but people from Madonna's past frequently comment on her exceptionally rebellious temperament as a child. She frequently discusses her stubborn nature, which she has from a young age. She became, and would continue to be, outspoken about people and issues that irritated her — even well-meaning youngsters. For example, one of Madonna's first recollections is of sitting in her parents' front yard in Michigan, being disciplined by her father for some minor misbehaviour. A two-year-old neighbour approached Madonna and presented her with a dandelion she had picked, wishing to befriend the cute little girl. Madonna responded by standing up, facing the child, and pushing her to the ground. "My first instinct," Madonna explained later, "was to lash out at someone who was more helpless than I." I saw an opportunity to retaliate against authority in her innocent eyes." The fact that the young guest offered her a dandelion did not appear to help matters. The adult Madonna went on to say she disliked dandelions because "they're weeds that run rampant, and I like things that are cultivated."

Despite being the third of six children, Madonna quickly learned how to keep a certain level of attention on her. In order to stay the centre point in a bustling household, she would, for example, adopt techniques inspired by the movies she binge-watched on television, such as jumping on top of a table at the drop of a hat and performing a Shirley Temple-style performance. She would add "a personal touch" at the end of her impromptu show by lifting up her dress and flashing her underpants. This bit of mischief was always a hit, delighting both young and old alike. The youngster appeared to be learning that a little flare paired with a little showmanship may go a long way toward satisfying people. Of course, the mature Madonna would combine these qualities to great effect in her professional career years later.

***

The terrible and unexpected death of Madonna's adored mother at the age of thirty was almost definitely the defining incident of her youth - the one that would have the biggest influence in shaping her into the woman she would become.

After her mother was diagnosed with breast cancer, Nonnie and her siblings watched as she deteriorated over the course of a year. However, many months before her mother died, Nonnie, then five, began to observe changes in her conduct and demeanour, albeit she didn't grasp the severe causes for such changes. Her mother had always been a meticulous homemaker, but following her diagnosis, she became weary easily and was unable to keep up with the housekeeping she had previously done with such dedication.

Madonna recalls her mother, weary, reclining on the couch in the middle of the afternoon. The young girl, seeking to play with her parents as she had always done, would jump on her back; her mother, too exhausted to move, would ignore her. When the small girl sensed that something dreadful was about to happen, she would pound fiercely on her mother's back and sob, "Why are you doing this? Stop acting like this! Be the person you used to be. "Come play with me!"

Madonna's mother, no doubt, was at a loss to convey to her terrified daughter the reality of her daughter's severe medical condition. She'd probably start crying because she was terrified and helpless, and her daughter would respond by compassionately wrapping her arms around her. "I remember feeling stronger than she was," Madonna said. "I was so small, but I felt like she was a child." After that, I stopped torturing her. "I believe it accelerated my maturation."

Madonna's mother was eventually admitted to a hospital. Once there, she tried to have a cheerful tone, usually smiling and cracking jokes for her visiting children. She knew she was dying, but she didn't want her children to know. "I remember that right before she died, she asked for a hamburger," Madonna remarked. "She wanted to eat a hamburger because she hadn't eaten anything in a long time." "I thought [her choice of a hamburger for her meal] was very amusing." Later that day, however, Madonna's father informed her that her mother had died. She couldn't realise the magnitude of the tragedy at first, and as she described it, "I kept waiting for her to come back." We never really talked about it [she and her father]. "I suppose we should have."

Madonna was only five years old when her mother died on December 1, 1963, and the impact on her was almost definitely immense. She lost her mother during a time when she was developing her identity and beliefs as a young girl. She needed a mother then, and she would always need one.

According to one view on childhood loss, the earlier the age, the greater the influence and the longer the impact. The age of five is a pivotal one. A five-year-old child may easily feel victimised by events, and may even believe that he or she should have had some influence over them. Certainly, Madonna's anger over losing her mother would be exceedingly tough for a five-year-old to bear. Some people will never be able to accept such a loss at such a young age, at least not without extensive therapy.

Following her meteoric rise to fame, Madonna said, "We are all wounded in one way or another by something in our lives, and then we spend the rest of our lives reacting to it or dealing with it or trying to turn it into something else." Madonna's grief over her mother's death "left me with a certain kind of loneliness and an incredible longing for something." "If I hadn't had that emptiness, I wouldn't have been so driven," she remarked. Her death had a lot to do with me stating, when I got over my heartbreak, that if I can't have my mother, I'm going to be incredibly strong. "I'm going to look after myself."

Madonna and her sisters would experience tremendous sadness when their mother's vivid memories faded away. They'd look at images of her and conclude that she resembled Anne Sexton, the Pulitzer Prize-winning poet of the 1960s who wrote about despair and suicide in works like To Bedlam and Part Way Back and Live or Die. This could explain Madonna's great interest in poetry. (Madonna has also mentioned Sylvia Plath as a poet she admires, which goes beyond most people's perception of Madonna as superficial. In fact, many of her songs are inspired by art, poetry, philosophy, and several religions.)

The young Madonna not only learned to care for herself, but she also cared for her brothers and sisters. She was eager to take on the maternal role with her siblings as the oldest female. Indeed, her brother Martin recalls Madonna not only feeding the younger children but also ensuring that they were properly clothed for school. "I didn't resent having to raise my brothers and sisters as much as I resented the fact that I didn't have my mother," she said. Actually, she didn't have to raise her siblings alone since her father hired a series of housekeepers... all of whom eventually quit rather than have to put up with the rambunctious Ciccone clan. Madonna and her siblings always resisted anyone who was brought into the house to take the place of their loving mother. Madonna was content to continue in the role of surrogate mother if it meant keeping other women out of her father's life (and having him all to herself). "Like all young girls," Madonna would explain, "I was madly in love with my father and didn't want to lose him." I lost my mother, but I became my mother... and my father became mine."

"I saw a very lonely girl who was searching for something," she once said in an interview with Vanity Fair about her childhood. "Seeking a mother figure." I wasn't rebellious in the traditional sense; I cared about excelling at something. I didn't shave beneath my arms or use makeup. But I worked hard and received decent grades. I rarely smoked marijuana, though I'm sure I did on occasion. I was an outcast and a rebel who wanted to satisfy my father and obtain straight A's. "I aspired to be somebody."

Because her mother's death had left such profound emotional wounds on her, the young Madonna was scared of losing her father as well. She would climb into bed in the middle of the night with just her father, as she had done a few years before with both of her parents. The young girl was plagued by repeated nightmares, and she could only fall asleep quietly and safely if she knew her father was nearby. She would never again allow herself to feel as abandoned as she had when her mother died, no doubt because of the grief she felt. Madonna would have to be strong for herself since she had always been afraid of weakness, particularly her own.

2. Confusing Times

In 1966, three years after Madonna's mother died, Tony Ciccone began a love relationship with Joan Gustafson, one of the Ciccones' many housekeepers. Much to Madonna's chagrin, the two married soon after. Perhaps it was about this time that Madonna began to display unresolved resentment toward her father, which would linger for decades.

The austere, blonde Gustafson was quite the opposite to Madonna's sweet, olive-skinned mother. Whereas Madonna's mother was laid-back and kind, Joan was a strict disciplinarian — or attempted to be. None of the kids ever paid attention to anything she said. The young Madonna also appeared to be struggling to adjust to no longer being the female leader of the household. She refused to address the new Mrs. Ciccone as "Mother," as her father had demanded.

When Madonna's career was just getting started in the early 1980s, she talked a lot about how her life had changed after her father remarried. She didn't despise her stepmother, she clarified; she just couldn't accept her in place of her own mother. Madonna, true to her sensational personality, would subsequently exaggerate any conflict between stepmother and stepchild for the press by claiming she always felt unloved and undesired, "always like Cinderella."

Madonna would also recount how the new Mrs. Ciccone once bloodied her nose in a violent altercation — a turn of events that Madonna said made her happy since it allowed her to skip Sunday worship for a change.

According to Madonna, another major "wicked stepmother" indignity inflicted on her by Joan was her insistence on Madonna and her sisters wearing matching clothing, robbing Madonna of the individuality she so treasured. Madonna remarked that wearing school uniforms was terrible enough, but dressing exactly like her sisters was torment.

Even at this young age, Madonna learnt to be creative with her style while seeking to assert her own personality — whether that meant shredding her clothes or turning them inside out while Joan wasn't around. Madonna would often wear old rags in her unkempt hair to distinguish herself from her younger sisters.

No matter how much Madonna despised the situation, it appeared that the new Mrs. Ciccone was here to stay. Joan as well as

Madonna would often speak of Tony Ciccone with affection, perhaps realising the obvious link between her capacity to attain success, maintain a competitive edge, and observing her father's own work ethic: "One thing my father was with us was very solid," she has stated. "He was very dependable in that way; he never confused me." He didn't preach one thing and then live another. He was always true to his word. He was a man of great character. And constancy was crucial, especially because I didn't have a mother."

Madonna had always relished receiving the benefits of hard effort; she liked to win. Tony had a habit of giving each of his children fifty cents for every A on their report card; Madonna always got the most As. She was naturally intelligent, an excellent student who seemed to be aware of the necessity of planning for her future. "That bitch never had to study," Martin, her brother, chuckles. "Never. She received all A's. I used to get up and study all the time, but my mind was elsewhere. I did it because I had to, but I didn't enjoy it. She did it because she knew it would propel her forward." Madonna also recalled the accolades she received for her A grades, adding, "I was really competitive, and my brothers and sisters despised me for it." Every report card, I made the most money."

All of the Ciccone children were encouraged to play a classical instrument in addition to their academic pursuits and domestic tasks.

Madonna was assigned to the piano, despite her aversion to it. Her area was racially diverse, and with that cultural influence at work, she was more interested in the local Motown sound than classical piano. Diana Ross and the Supremes, Ronnie Spector, and Stevie Wonder were her idols.

Madonna swiftly persuaded her father to let her forgo her monotonous piano lessons in order to pursue more interesting (for her) pastimes such as tap and jazz dance, as well as baton twirling.

***

She had her First Communion in 1966, and when she was confirmed a year later, she added the name Veronica to her birth name. "I took the name Veronica," she says, "because she wiped the face of Jesus." You weren't intended to assist Jesus Christ on his route to the Crucifixion. She was not hesitant to come out and wipe his perspiration and assist him. So I stole her name since I liked her for doing that. "There was also Mary Magdalene," she recalls of biblical women who affected her. "She was regarded as a fallen woman because she had slept with men." But Jesus said everything was all right. "Jesus and Mary Magdalene, I think they got it on."

Madonna would employ Catholic iconography as part of her sensual wardrobe early in her career and then give juicy comments to journalists, such as the oft-quoted "crucifixes are sexy because there's a naked man on them." As an adult, Madonna would adopt one of her most frequently used and successful "shock" formulas: imbuing a respected, sacred image with entirely inappropriate sexual overtones, making even the mere concept of the total package completely taboo. She rapidly discovered that shocking words like "crucifixes are sensual because Jesus was so sexy, like a movie star, almost" raised eyebrows, got her recognized, and got people talking about her as a sexual revolutionary. Combining religion with sex was a winning combination for controversy. While simple to prepare, by the second or third time, it became a very obvious trick. Nonetheless, because the public remained stunned, and even delighted and amused by her insights, Madonna repeated the formula frequently — on talk programs, in music videos, and in some of her songs.

In truth, many of Madonna's sarcastic perspectives on Catholicism (considered blasphemous by some more faithful observers) stem from a deep resentment of the church. Perhaps she felt so strongly that the orthodoxy that surrounds her had failed her down that she acted provocatively as a way of mocking it. Some thought she had rejected God because He had done something dreadful to her - taken away her mother. She seemed to repeatedly challenge Him to retaliate against her as she continued to act in ways that may be considered sacrilegious, at least to a religious person.

As an adult, Madonna would blame the church's strict, puritanical, suffering-based beliefs for many of the Ciccone children's difficulties. "My older brothers were incredibly rebellious," she went on to say. "They got involved with drugs and got into trouble with the cops." My brother fled away and became a Moonie. Me? I developed into an overachiever. 'I don't care if I have to live on the street, and I don't care if I have to eat garbage,' I told myself. 'I'll take care of it.'"

The way Madonna was impacted by her mother's rather passionate — and perplexing — devotion must have contributed to her religious ambiguity. "Catholicism is a very masochistic religion," the grown-up Madonna would say. "I also witnessed my mother doing things that deeply affected me." During Lent, she would kneel on uncooked rice and pray. She slept on wire hangers. She was deeply devout, almost swooning over it. If my aunt came over to my house wearing zipped-up jeans, my mother would cover all the statues so they couldn't view such a display. She then aimed the holy images at the wall."

Madonna's family relocated to 2036 Oklahoma Street in Rochester Hills, Michigan, an affluent town near the exclusive Detroit suburb of Bloomfield Hills, when she was about eleven years old. It was at that point that she began to consider becoming a nun. "I wanted a pious way of life," she told the author in 1983. "But I was at odds with everything." The more it repulsed me, the more I wanted it, like if I were attempting to conquer something. I believe the church ruined my life. It pushed me to be more competitive. It made me fearful of failing. It caused a slew of issues, many of which I'm sure I'm unaware of. I'm truly scared to go into hypnosis because I'm afraid of what I'll learn about my Catholic upbringing!"

Those nuns at St. Andrew's Elementary School had always piqued Madonna's interest. She would try to capture them in their "natural" surroundings by sneaking looks through the convent windows. She pondered what they looked like without their habits and if they even had hair. Carol Belager, a childhood friend, recalls Madonna peeking through convent windows with her.

"Oh my God, they do have hair," Madonna said to Carol as the two girls snooped on Sister Mary Christina.

"Let's go now," Carol suggested hesitantly.

"No, she's getting ready to strip," Madonna exclaimed enthusiastically. "I want to see what she looks like naked."

Carol yanked Madonna aside before she could witness her first naked nun.

Madonna's ambivalence about the teachings of the Catholic Church is especially paradoxical given that Catholicism appears to have provided her with the ability to transcend her own fears. The concept urged her to address periods of tremendous self-weakness, when she suspected she wasn't good enough, talented enough, or pretty enough... those times when she most needed to rely on faith to overcome emotions of inadequacy. It also instilled in her the severe sense of self-discipline required to face the many challenges she would undoubtedly face on the way to celebrity.

3. Losing Her Virginity

Despite feeling virtually suffocated by a rigorous religious setting, Madonna's talent blossomed and, on occasion, she would find innovative methods to unleash it. Madonna's father smoldered when he witnessed his adolescent daughter bumping and grinding in public. He then grounded her for two weeks. "I don't know what she was thinking," he admits now. "Besides the fact that she wanted to shock everyone."

Madonna found several hobbies at Rochester Adams High School to keep herself in the public eye. As a cheerleader, she experienced what it was like to perform in front of large crowds. She was then given the opportunity to put some of the tactics she had learned as a child to the test in front of her grateful family, but on a larger, and possibly more critical, audience.

Karen Craven, who was on Madonna's cheerleading squad, recounts the day the squad was supposed to form a standard "human pyramid" during a game break. "Vaulted up to the top and did a little flip," Madonna recalls. When the teenager's skirt flew up, the audience let out a collective gasp. Nancy Ryan Mitchell, a guidance counsellor, says, "From a distance, she appeared to be naked." She was, however, wearing a pair of flesh-coloured tights. It was surprising, to say the least. That, however, was Madonna.

Madonna was also active in the theatre, appearing in shows such as My Fair Lady, Cinderella, The Wizard of Oz, and Godspell. She'd discover what it was like to delight an audience on the high school stage, to stand in the spotlight and accept a crowd's warm applause. "She liked it," a former classmate, Clara Bonell, said. "I saw her in Godspell, and I remember her crying as the audience stood for the curtain call." I believe that the sense of acceptance was what she most valued and desired. I believe she thought she didn't get it at home from her father, who was, as far as I recall, unsupportive. So, if she could get it from an audience, that would be great."

Beverly Gibson, her theatre teacher, adds, "When she was in the spotlight, she was pure magic." People were drawn to her; you couldn't take your gaze away from her. People who become renowned are frequently described as wallflowers. You may hear their friends and professors remark things like, 'Oh, I would never have imagined her to become famous.' Not the case with Madonna. She couldn't possibly be anything other than famous at anything. "I'd watch her on stage with that vibrant personality and charisma and think, 'Oh, my, it's inevitable, isn't it?'"

"In high school, Madonna was a nonconformist," says Tanis Rozelle, a former classmate. "Unlike the other girls, she and her sister Melanie did not shave their armpits." That was thought to be unusual. Both of them had thick tufts of hair coming from beneath their armpits. It sparked some debate at first, but people eventually accepted it. Madonna stated that she does not shave because she did not want to be stereotyped as a regular suburban American girl. She stated that she did not want to remove something natural from her body. "It didn't stop her from raising her arms high and cheering, even when she was wearing a sleeveless uniform," Tanis recalls. "It didn't stop her from being popular with the boys." She was quite attractive, and the males adored her."

Madonna lost her virginity to seventeen-year-old Russell Long during her first year of high school, in December 1973, at the age of fifteen. She claims she had several sexual encounters earlier to this period, when she was eight years old, but no intercourse. "All of my sexual experiences when I was young were with girls," she said. "I mean, those sleepover parties weren't for nothing." Same-sex experimentation is, in my opinion, quite natural. You become quite inquisitive, and then there's your girlfriend, who is staying the night with you, and it occurs."

"She wanted her first time having real sex to be something special," Russell Long recalls now. "We had a date — a movie and burgers — and afterward we drove my very cool, blue 1966 Caddy back to my parents' place."

Long recalls being worried about the signs Madonna was sending him — it was evident she wanted to be intimate with him — but he didn't have to worry about initiating anything. She was the one who made the first move. "Are we going to do it, or not?" she wondered as she took off her bra.

"I guess so," Russell responded quickly.

"Well, then, c'mon," she urged. "Do it!"

Years later, she would reflect, "Even after I had my first kiss, I still felt like a virgin." "I didn't lose my virginity until I was confident in what I was doing."

Long claims that after their first meeting at his parents' house, they preferred the backseat of his Cadillac for future rendezvous. "My friends called it 'the Passion Wagon,'" he remembers.

"She didn't mind that everyone knew we were having sex. Many girls her age would have felt ashamed, or would have rather that no one knew. Madonna is not one of them. She was pleased with it and said it made her feel more like a woman. She felt at ease with her body and didn't mind being seen naked. She just appeared at ease with everything."

"I liked my body when I was growing up," Madonna reportedly told a reporter, "and I wasn't ashamed of it." I liked boys and was not put off by them. Perhaps it stems from growing up with brothers and sharing a bathroom. In high school, the lads had the wrong impression of me. They confused boldness with promiscuity. They turn on you when they don't get what they desire. I had a phase where all the girls thought I was loose and all the boys thought I was a nymphomaniac. My boyfriend was the first boy I ever slept with, and we'd been dating for a long time."

"She wasn't like most of the other students," Russell Long remembers. "There was a group of kids who were just the odd ones, the ones the majority of the students thought were creepy." Madonna was among them. She didn't fit in with the rest of the students; instead, she was one of those youngsters on the outskirts, smirking at everyone else.

"However, I found her to be quite sensitive," he goes on to say. "We talked for a long time about her mother and how much she missed her. We also talked about the conflict she had with her father. By high school, she was rebelling against him in every manner, and she seemed so upset at him that I didn't understand why. 'What do you think he'd do if he found out we were having sex?' she'd ask. Do you think it would frighten him?' And I'd answer, 'Hell, sure, it would terrify him out.' Then she'd respond, 'Well, then, maybe I should tell him.' 'No, Madonna!' I'd say. He's going to murder me.' But neither my safety nor her privacy were on her mind. She wanted to be able to blow his head, to stun him. More than that, she wanted to irritate him in every way she could." Long and Madonna's relationship lasted six months.

Russell Long, a trucker for United Parcel Service, is still married with children and resides in Michigan. "I wonder if he still loves me," Madonna pondered at one point. Then, as if waking up, she answered her own question. "Oh, of course he does!"

"Sure I do," Russell Long says now. "Even if she hadn't become famous, I would never have forgotten her." She was exceptional."

4. Busting Out

By the beginning of 1979, Madonna, who would turn twenty-one that year, recognized that she would have to wait another five years before being accepted into a large touring dance company. She felt the answer to her problem was obvious: she needed to diversify, broaden her horizons, and possibly even change her vision if she wanted to survive in New York.

Madonna, ever loyal to her character, would not waste time planning her next move. She required a vehicle that would allow her tremendous magnetism to shine. She needed a venue, a forum. Madonna began appearing naked for painting lessons in order to make extra money. She'd heard it was a simple way to generate money, and as she later said, "I was so broke and desperate, I would have done almost anything." And I thought it may give me a new direction, that I could become a model. "No one knows."

Madonna then chose to pose naked for photographers who had advertised in the publications and newspapers she read in order to supplement her income. On February 12, 1979, Martin Schreiber, who was teaching a course for the New School in Greenwich Village at the time, paid her thirty dollars to pose naked for ninety minutes. When she received her payment, she signed the release form as Madonna Louise.

Meanwhile, Madonna's unique blend of flair, daring, and personality drew prominent individuals to her like a magnet. Norris Burroughs noticed her while she was spinning around in the middle of the dance floor at a party. "It was the winter of 1979," says Burroughs. "I remember she was wearing leopard tights and there were people all around her, but she was getting centre stage despite the fact that the house was packed with dancers." It felt like a rite, as if she were dancing in a ring of fire. So there we were, me, my friends, and everyone else, singing and dancing to the Village People's 'YMCA,' and Madonna was right in the heart of it all, centre stage. She was this incredible and exciting-looking creature with wild hair and a lot of sexual energy just itching to burst forth and make an impression. I was extremely surprised. So I had no choice but to approach her.

Burroughs turned to Madonna during one of their lovemaking sessions and remarked, "In a year, we'll look back on this time and appreciate it even more, won't we?"

"Hmmm," Madonna murmured, her voice hesitant. "Interesting," she said, her smile deceptive.

Burroughs slept peacefully with his arms about her, knowing — as he would later concede — that these tender moments would be few and far between.

So far, Madonna's career had been propelled forward by a series of coincidental events that had introduced her to prominent people who could assist her in achieving her goals. She gladly seized the possibilities that were provided to her, then pushed forth and upward without much apparent thanks or nostalgia, never looking back. It was the way it had been up until now, and it would be a pattern of her life for years to come. Despite the fact that her romance with Norris Burroughs lasted only three months, it did usher Madonna into the next chapter of her life. Burroughs introduced her to pals Dan and Ed Gilroy, who had created the Breakfast Club, at a gathering at his house on May 1, 1979.

Madonna and Dan Gilroy hit it off right away. As the evening came to a close, she questioned, "Well, aren't you going to kiss me?" She took him by the tie, drew him close, and kissed him deeply on the lips as he contemplated the topic. Then she lightly smacked him twice on the same cheek. She went away after winking at him.

"Before I knew it, she was done with me and was with Dan," Norris Burroughs would recall years later. Dan began teaching her how to play instruments right away. She learnt to play the guitar as well as the organ. They put her behind the drums for a while, but she soon wanted to sing."

Madonna soon found herself living with Dan and his brother in a decrepit and boarded-up synagogue in Corona, Queens, which they would use as both a practice hall and a living place — she was now a member of the Breakfast Club.

Dan was enthralled by Madonna. "You make love like a man," he told her afterward, according to a recollection. "You're quite assertive. Uninhibited."

"Does that scare you?" she inquired.

"No," he replied. "It turns me on."

"I've always wanted to be a guy," she admits. "I just want to take off my shirt in the middle of the street like a construction worker." "I enjoy the freedom."

"I like you," he said.

"I know," she said as she kissed him on the lips.

"Dan and Eddie both sang, and sometimes she sang, and then they would sing behind her," recounts Norris Burroughs. "She eventually wanted to sing more." She had given up on dancing, I believe, once she joined the band and became connected with Dan. She simply desired to work less as a dancer and more with the band. She took it all in, learning everything Dan could tell her about rock music, including how to play and sing it. She simply desired more...

"More" was something Madonna had always desired, and it appeared that she was beginning to wonder if singing was not the way to obtain it. "With the Breakfast Club, she found her muse medium, she found the best vessel for her drive as a rock performer," producer

Steve Bray, who had known Madonna in Michigan and caught up with her again in Manhattan around this time, remembers. She sang and played guitar in the band. I've always believed she'd make an excellent rhythm guitarist. She'd break items all around her by dancing on the tabletops. She'd douse herself with champagne. "She was a fantastic, wild child."Dan had a lot to teach her. He adored her. They seemed to get along well, in my opinion. But I knew it was only a matter of time."

Madonna continued to comb the pages of industry periodicals like Backstage, Show Business, and Variety for job openings each week. "I saw an ad in the newspaper for this French singing star, Patrick Hernandez," she told a Playboy journalist in September 1985. He had a single called 'Born to Be Alive.' His record label [Columbia Records] was attempting to put up an act to accompany him on a world tour, and they were looking for girls to sing backup vocals and dance. It was going to be a large gala show. I imagined myself dancing and singing and travelling throughout the world – I'd never been outside of America. So I went to the tryouts, and after they were finished, they told me that they didn't want me for Patrick Hernandez, but instead wanted to bring me to Paris and make me a disco star."

Madonna expressed her regret at having to leave Dan so abruptly, describing him as "one of the most generous men she'd ever known." "I learned a lot from you, Dan," she told him. "However, it is time for me to depart. "And if that makes me a bitch, so be it," she ended. Hurt, Dan readily agreed with her evaluation of herself: "Yes, she was a bitch," he replied. He later admitted that he loved her and thought they had "something going on." He couldn't believe she'd leave him, "especially after everything we'd shared."

Madonna, at twenty, travelled to Paris in May 1979 with producers Jean Vanloo and Jean-Claude Pallerin, who promised to treat her properly, give her "fabulous foods," and "get me a vocal coach."

"They did all of that," she recalled to one reporter. It was a lot of fun. I had a fantastic apartment. I've never had it so good in my life. I was chauffeured everywhere. They were going to nurture my talent and find me a vehicle."

"They took me to Paris and introduced me to awful French boys, took me to expensive restaurants, and dragged me around to show their friends what they had found in the gutters of New York," she told another reporter. I'd have tantrums, and they'd give me money to make me happy. "I was in a bad mood."

"So I went into my rebel mode and gave away my money and started hanging around with bums," she went on to say. "Oh, how I longed for New York. I despised France and all things French. If they weren't going to do anything for me, I wanted to return to New York, where I thought I could help myself. Because I didn't have a contract, I told them I needed to return home to see a sick friend. They agreed, summoned a limousine, and had me dropped off at the airport. They inquired as to when you will return. I told them it would be two weeks. I never went back after that. [In 1985], I learned that they are still looking for me. "You poor dears."

It speaks a lot about Madonna's nature that she would enthusiastically return to New York, where she at least felt in charge of her destiny, even when she had nothing going on. In France, her aspirations would have been realised by a few record producers she didn't even know very well. In New York, however, she was in charge. She was willing to take a risk, betting that her own imagination and inventiveness would propel her to the next level of her career.

Madonna ran into Patrick Hernandez at the rehearsal hall where he was putting together his disco act before leaving Paris for her "brief stay" in New York. "Success is yours today, honey," she said to him, "but it will be all mine tomorrow."

In 1999, Madonna asked a reporter, "What the hell ever happened to Patrick Hernandez, anyway?"

5. Certain Sacrifices

Madonna and her friend Whitley Setrakian discussed her thrilling trip to Europe three weeks after she returned home in August 1979. "She was living in a real hellhole in New York," Whitley remembers. "But she called it home, and so we lay on the floor on a futon and she told me this incredible story about how she had gone to Paris on the Concorde, how she hated it there, and how she turned around and came back." I was taken aback by how matter-of-factly she delivered it to me. This was a huge thing to me. But she seemed unconcerned about it.

After auditioning for the films Footloose and Fame (but not being cast in either), the twenty-one-year-old Madonna submitted images and a handwritten letter/résumé to amateur filmmaker Stephen Jon Lewicki. She was responding to his Backstage post, which stated, in part, "Wanted: Woman for low-budget film." Type of dominatrix."

When Lewicki opened the mail, he discovered Madonna's résumé, two 3X5 colour photographs, one 8X10 black-and-white photograph, and a handwritten three-page letter that he still keeps. Madonna, who began by saying she had recently "returned from Europe," went on to say, "I was born and raised in Detroit, Michigan, where I began my career in petulance and precociousness." When I was fifteen, I started attending dance classes on a regular basis, listening to baroque music, and gradually but steadily developing a hate for my classmates, teachers, and high school in general. My drama class was the one exception."

He goes on to say, "Suddenly, here was a girl who I thought had some interesting possibilities." He also noted that they were born in the same year. But it wasn't just that particular coincidence — or, perhaps, omen — that piqued his interest in her. "There was something about her photos that made me want to meet her," Lewicki remarked. She was sexy but not vulgar in them. I'd gotten a lot of images and messages from ladies who appeared to be whores but wanted to be actresses, and actresses who wanted to be whores. Madonna's images, on the other hand, were unique. In one, she was applying lipstick with her pinkie finger while sitting in a bus stop, I suppose. There was something alluring about it, but it also had a fragility, an innocence that captivated me. I was determined to meet her. So we convened in Washington Square Park."

Madonna arrived with a tight red miniskirt and her cocky, self-assured demeanour. "You'd think she had a great résumé and a lot of experience based on the way she acted," Lewicki recalls with a smile. "She was tough."

Lewicki cast Madonna in his low-budget, one-hour film about the bizarre happenings between a downtown dominatrix named Bruna (Madonna) and her suburban, outcast boyfriend, Dashiel (Jeremy Pattnosh). When Bruna is raped in a diner's bathroom, she and her boyfriend hire "sex slaves" to conduct a satanic human sacrifice on the rapist. "At no time did I ever ask her to take her clothes off," Lewicki recalls. "It just evolved while she was performing the scene." She felt at ease with her body, with nudity. "It's not pornographic at all; it's very passionate and interesting," he explains. "We began filming in October 1979, and we had a lot of fun; she was always up, full of energy, and able to improvise." Actually, I had a crush on her. We insulted and cut each other down a lot. That's how you feel about Madonna. When she attacks you and you insult her back, she knows you love her.

Many actresses' first low-budget films are rarely memorable, and Madonna's is no exception, with its ending depicting a human sacrifice. The screenplay is confused, the sound is subpar, and everyone's performance, including Madonna's, is overblown and incompetent, if possibly unwittingly prophetic. Nonetheless, the film is well-intended.

Despite the low-budget nature of her work, Madonna, with her natural brunette hair cut in a close-cropped style, was already acting like the celebrity she would become in just a few short years. Russell Lome, who starred in a hot love scene with Madonna, was stunned by the inexperienced actress's boldness.

***

By the beginning of 1980, Madonna's instincts were telling her that her future was not in film, at least not yet, and certainly not in dance. At this point, she reconnected with her ex-boyfriend Dan Gilroy, who couldn't resist reintroducing her... into his life, and also into the Breakfast Club. However, her burgeoning ambition soon prompted her to clash with both Gilroy brothers. While they perceived her as just another member of the band, she felt herself as the primary attraction and so desired to sing more leads, especially after another female (Angie Smits) joined the band as a bass player. She liked Angie, but she couldn't help but see her as a competitor; she didn't appreciate sharing the stage with another woman. As the weeks grew into months, Dan became increasingly annoyed by Madonna's habit of overshadowing him and the other band members. She always had a lot of other males set up for her, and each one had a certain function in her life. She was done with me for good when she was done with me that time."

Madonna appeared to be ready to move on once more. Dan Gilroy had given her a home to live, the security of being in a relationship with someone who actually loved her, knowledge of some musical instruments, and a taste of what it was like to sing in front of an audience with a support band. She was now inspired to form her own band, create her own sound, and promote her own persona... without Dan Gilroy.

"I know he was pretty brokenhearted," Norris Burroughs, the man who introduced Dan to Madonna, says. "He wasn't the type of guy who put much stock in relationships, but Madonna did a number on him." They had a sense of inevitability about them, the way she went to Paris and you thought it was done, then she returned and you realised it wasn't over at all, that it had just begun again. I'm not sure if she was using him or not. Only she would be aware of this. But it all seemed extremely star-crossed to me at the time."

Madonna teamed up with her Michigan boyfriend, percussionist Steve Bray, soon after leaving the Gilroys' synagogue/studio/living quarters. The two met at the University of Michigan in 1976, while Bray was working as a waiter at the Blue Frog bar on Church Street in Ann Arbor, which was popular with many university students. He was also a drummer for an R&B band and, according to Madonna, "the first guy I ever allowed to buy me a drink [a gin and tonic]." He was irresistibly attractive." Bray invited Madonna to accompany him across Michigan as he and his band performed in small bars after getting romantically engaged with her. They stayed friends after their romance ended. Bray later relocated to New York.

Madonna had decided that she wanted to pursue a musical career in New York and wanted to be engaged in it 24 hours a day. She spent the next year creating songs and singing locally around New York with a small backup band that included Steve Bray on drums, feeling herself bursting at the seams with imagination and invention. Because Bray needed somewhere to live, the two agreed to move into the Music Building, a West Side Manhattan conglomeration of offices and rehearsal studios on Eighth Avenue, and just sleep in the studios of any of the tenants who would consent to such a thing — and some would. "The Music Building," Bray says, "was close to the Port Authority Bus Terminal." There were a lot of singers and bands there, just trying to figure out their music in practice halls and studios. It was a nice spot, extremely artsy. You could almost taste the inventiveness. We loved it since just being in the ambiance was energising. Our band was hot, and it was only getting hotter."

Despite the uncertainty surrounding the group's identity, Madonna's self-assurance and perspective for the future remained unshakeable. However, for someone who had never performed before, she had developed the ego of a great — and, in some respects, challenging — celebrity. Bray says, "She wanted to call the band 'Madonna.'" That was just too much for me."

"But it makes a lot of sense," Madonna told Steve Bray during lunch at Howard Johnson's in Times Square. "See, there was this group named Patti LaBelle and the Blue Belles. And when they recreated themselves, they called themselves Labelle, after the group's leader."

Bray absorbed this knowledge. "So, what are you saying?" he inquired. "That you're the leader of this band?"

"Why, no, not at all," Madonna replied, her tone pleasant. "You're the brains, Steve. You're a musical genius. Me? "Why, I'm just the star."

"Forget it, Emmy," he told her. "It sounds too Catholic, anyway." 'Madonna?' No, I don't think so."

Even now, Madonna admits that she was surprised by the group's unwillingness to be called after her. Why didn't her coworkers grasp the obvious reality — at least her reality — that she was their meal ticket? While she may have believed she was acting in their and her own best interests, the rest of the band mistook her for selfishness. In the end, the group settled on the moniker "Emmy," with Dan and Ed Gilroy as front men, Madonna on lead vocals, former Breakfast Club member Gary Burke on bass, Brian Syms on lead guitar, and Steve Bray on drums. Madonna says, "We played, we sang, we went all over New York just trying to make money, which never happened." It was less enjoyable than I had planned."

Frustrated, Madonna decided that the constraints of being a member of a band had already begun to damage her actual identity as a performer. "It was too confining," she would later recall. "I had some thoughts. It's impossible to have ideas in a band. Why bother if I can't express myself?"

6. Madonna: The Debut Album

Madonna's debut album, released in July, might have been from any of the dance performers who passed through pop music's revolving door in 1983. The eight-song collection didn't give even a hint of the huge superstardom to which it would be the entrée, but it did give a clear indication of what the Madonna movement's pioneers, such as Camille Barbone and Steve Bray, saw in her.

Reggie Lucas had made a name for himself in the R&B music industry with songwriting partner James Mtume, producing a string of hit records for acts like Roberta Flack and Donny Hathaway ("The Closer I Get to You"), Phyllis Hyman ("You Know How to Love Me"), and, most notably, Stephanie Mills ("Whatcha' Gonna Do with My Lovin," "Put Your Body in It," and "Never Knew Love Like This Before"

Mtume and Lucas recorded and produced one album (In Search of the Rainbow Seekers) for the Epic label under the moniker Mtume before splitting up. While Mtume the band was working on their 1983 R&B hit "Juicy Fruit," Mtume's ex-partner was producing Madonna, an unknown white girl who lacked the voice of Stephanie Mills or any of the other singers he'd worked with in the past. When Madonna and Reggie Lucas started writing songs for her debut album, the process grew tedious. "She had her own way of wanting to do things," Lucas explains. "And I realised that. So we needed to get together every now and then."

Madonna had composed a song named "Lucky Star" (along with two others) that, combined with Reggie's piece "Borderline," seemed to be the ideal foundation for the album. However, Madonna was dissatisfied with Lucas' production after recording the three tracks. "It's just too much," she sighed at the moment. "Too many instruments, too much stuff going on."

"You have to let me do what I do," Reggie urged her, according to what he remembered saying later.

She made a lengthy expression. "However, I have some ideas." "I have ideas," Madonna argued. "I've been doing this for a long time, too."

"I know that," he admitted. "But, Madonna, when you bring in a producer, you have to let him do his job."

"Well, just don't get in my way," Madonna said, threateningly.

She apologised the next day.

Lucas didn't seem interested in rewriting the record to Madonna's demands after completing it. Instead, he moved on to another project as soon as possible, leaving Madonna to figure out what to do with her album. She opted to enlist the help of her partner, the renowned Jellybean Benitez, to remix a number of the tracks, notably the fluffy, danceable (but forgettable) "Lucky Star." Also included on the CD is a song Jellybean added at the last minute, "Holiday" (written by Curtis Hudson and Lisa Stevens of Pure Energy) and produced by Benitez.

At first glance, Madonna's album appeared to be a rebound project for Reggie Lucas, the type of job that a notable record producer does for the money and to keep himself busy. It looked especially so when word spread that he didn't want to finish the album Madonna's way. However, upon closer study, it was evident that the album was stocked with hit singles. Even if the songs never became famous, no one could deny that they were fantastic, well-crafted pop tunes that deserved to be heard. However, based on the chart performance of the album's first single, "Everybody," one would never have known. The rhythmic call-to-party reached No. 1 on Billboard's dance chart — a ranking determined more by a song's popularity in dance clubs than commercial sales — but stalled at No. 103 on the trade magazine's pop chart, the one, as they say in the industry, "that really counts."

The double-sided twelve-inch single that followed — the yearning "Burning Up" backed by the droning but urgent "Physical Attraction" — didn't chart at all on Billboard's pop chart, but did reach Number 1 on the dance chart, seemingly defining this young new singer as just another disposable post-disco dance act.

Then there was "Holiday."

The joyous, addictive hymn, written once again by young journeymen Chris Hudson and Lisa Stevens, caught fire almost immediately, first flying in dance clubs across the country — where audiences were already familiar with Madonna — and then pushing its way onto R&B and pop charts. Finally, the song reached No. 16 on the coveted Billboard pop singles chart, a victory for a rookie act.

Just as the market was getting ready for this new "dance act," Sire threw a curveball and released "Borderline." Reggie Lucas wrote the song, which was a sad piece with a particularly strong melodic lyric about a love that is never fully realised.

Perhaps it was Madonna's fluid, loving approach to lyrics that had more to say than "shake your booty," or the fact that audiences had grown accustomed to her tart voice; whatever the case, her vocals on "Borderline" sounded refined, capable, and expressive. The combination of a not-so-great but touching voice at the centre of Lucas' rich, glittering instrumentation brought the single as close to an old Motown production as a hit could get in the dance-music-driven 1980s.

"Borderline," together with "Holiday," were arguably two of the most crucial records in Madonna's formative years, and not just because they charted at Nos. 16 and 10, respectively. Rather, the singles were essential because they provided Madonna with two separate platforms inside the dance music structure. Most importantly, they gave the one-two punch that allowed "Lucky Star," which was brilliant in its simplicity and danceability and was the fourth single from Madonna's album, to reach No. 4.

Later, Madonna, who co-wrote five of the album's eight songs, referred to this debut as an "aerobics album," yet the songs were well timed. Despite a poor start, the album soon climbed the charts and, after a year of release, cracked the Top 10. It eventually sold four million copies in the United States and eight million globally.

Madonna and Erica Bell celebrated her new accomplishment with a bottle of champagne shortly after the album reached the Top 10. Erica remembers the talk as if it had happened just days before.

"I feel bad about some of the people who aren't with me, the ones I met along the way," Madonna remarked, looking melancholy.

"You mean, like Camille?" Erica inquired. "Yeah, like her and the others."

"Well, this is a tough business," Erica pointed out. "It's the people hangin' around the moment you become successful who get to celebrate with you . . . not the ones you met along the way."

Madonna concurred. "I guess so," she responded, clinking her champagne glass to Erica's. "Anyway, sentimentality is a weakness, don't you think?"

Erica remained silent.

"People hate me," Madonna observed.

"I know they do," Erica confirmed.

"Oh well," Madonna said, shrugging. "I did what I needed to do." At the very least, I still have you."

"That you do," Erica said, hugging her pal.

The almost magical way Madonna's recording career coincided with the burgeoning popularity of the music video art form was maybe the most perfect timing of her career. Teenagers at the time seemed to need idols. The disco period produced numerous successful tunes but few outstanding musicians in the 1970s. However, several music performers in the early 1980s gained popularity for the unique images they showed the television-watching public in song videos: Cyndi Lauper with shocking orange hair, crazy makeup, and thrift-store clothes; Boy George with heavy-lidded mascara eyes and a woman's wardrobe; and Prince with his androgynous sex appeal and Purple Rain ruffles. All three, as well as many others, including Michael Jackson — who helped to pioneer and spread the medium with his long-form "Thriller" video — benefitted from the three-minute star vehicles that videos provided.

No one, however, used the medium better or more effectively than Madonna. She borrowed extensively from the downtown street scene, nightclubbing, and legends such as Marilyn Monroe, and mixed in her own brand of straightforward sexuality for an early image that was simply unforgettable. Even with her bubble gum-sounding debut album, her appearance sparked plenty of controversy as she mixed sexuality and religion, wearing belly button-exposing T-shirts and rosary beads. Many people thought Madonna's usage of crucifixes was sacrilegious, yet the religious sign became an important aspect of the Madonna fashion fad. "I don't think she was looking for controversy by wearing the crucifix," says Mary Lambert, a controversial director who directed some of Madonna's music videos. "I believe it had significance for her — religious significance, mystic significance." Madonna is a deeply devout woman in her own right."

Susan McMillan of the Pro Family Media Coalition said of Madonna's appearance at the time, "Underwear as outerwear is only there to titillate men." And believe me when I say that some sicko seeing a fourteen-year-old girl strolling down the street in nothing but a lacy bra isn't going to stop and say, 'Excuse me, before I grab you, can we talk about what sort of message you're trying to make?'"

Of course, Madonna revealed the indignation she provoked in fundamentalists such as Susan McMillan. It was what she desired, what she toiled for... and what she knew would make her a pop phenomenon just as much as any music she could possibly produce. She anticipated that the more the press labelled her style as "trashy," the more vocal parental opposition to her appearance would be, encouraging rebellious children to mimic her. Young ladies, branded "wannabes" (as in "wannabe Madonna") by the press, began wearing cross earrings and fingerless gloves. They wore scarves and stockings in their wild hair, all of which Madonna popularised in her videos. Her achievement verified Madonna's childhood strategy for attracting attention: do something that would shock people and, if extreme enough, it will get them talking. She didn't mind what they were saying as long as it was something about her.

Madonna's image was selfish, rude, and sexual. Above all, the statement she was conveying with her image and attitude was a desire for fame and infamy. It wasn't false or staged, that's for sure. It was organic — she claimed she just pulled her outfits together from whatever she had in the closet and whatever cheap stuff she had found at thrift stores — and extremely relevant.

"Do you think my mother would be proud of me?" she asked Jellybean Benitez after the publication of her first album.

"Oh my God, Madonna, yes," he recalls responding. "Look at what you've accomplished. Take a look at what you've accomplished. "Any mother would be overjoyed."

Madonna grinned. "And my father?"

"Absolutely," Jellybean replied. "Tony is content. You're aware of it."

"Yeah, well," Madonna said, "not that it matters."

7. The Affair with Prince

Madonna, 26, and Sean Penn, 24, began dating shortly after their initial meeting on the production of the "Material Girl" video. "After the video shoot, I was over at a friend's house," he said. "And he had a quotation book." He took it up, opened it to a random page, and read: 'She had the innocence of a child and the wit of a man.' When I looked at my pal, he simply said, 'Go get her.' As a result, I did." However, Sean's life was complicated by the fact that Madonna was also seeing rock singer Prince at the time, whom she met backstage at the American Music Awards in Los Angeles on January 28, 1985. He wasn't her type, and it's unclear why Madonna was interested in him, other than the fact that she admired him as a musician and undoubtedly wanted to know what made him tick.

Prince (actual name Prince Rogers Nelson) was and still is an unusual man known for his curiously bashful manner in private and wild sexuality on stage, parading around in bikini briefs and high heels. Prince declined to speak during an interview with the author the same year he met Madonna. Instead, he sat motionless in his chair in front of a meal of Chinese food and spent the entire evening fiddling with shrimp fried rice, his face glum. He would either nod affirmatively or shake his head negatively in response to each question. He left without saying goodbye after the interview was complete. "And that, my friend, is Prince," Prince's spokesman explained.

As their first date, Prince invited Madonna to one of his Los Angeles gigs. She was supposed to travel to New York to begin rehearsals for her own concert tour, but she opted to postpone that trip for a few days so she could spend time with the rock singer. He picked her up in a white extended limousine on the night of his concert and drove her to the Forum, where he was performing. Madonna subsequently revealed that she was surprised to discover that the little rock singer smelled strongly like lavender, "like a woman," she noted. "I had the impression I was in the presence of Miss Elizabeth Taylor." He smells strongly of lavender. It actually turned me on."

T. L. Ross, a friend of Prince's, observed, "I heard she was pretty aggressive, that the poor little guy had to fight her off." She was tough. He said she had the power of ten ladies." Prince didn't want to tire himself with Madonna because he had a show that evening. He advised them to wait.

Following the show, the two went out into the nightlife of Los Angeles, eventually ending up at the Marquis Hotel in Westwood for a party with Prince's entourage. When Prince hopped up onto a table and began to strip, the crowd became raucous. Madonna joined him on the table for a passionate bump-and-grind, her shoulders swinging up and down, her body quivering. The celebration ended at five a.m., and Prince and Madonna retired to Prince's private chamber, arm in arm and almost holding each other up.

The couple continued to meet each other for the next two months, despite the fact that they didn't appear to have much in common other than their status as renowned performers. He was secretive and shy, but she was open and honest. Fortunately, they both adored Marilyn Monroe. Madonna claimed she couldn't wait to view his collection of memorabilia when he informed her his home was adorned with posters of the blonde movie beauty.

Prince rented up the entire Yamashiro hilltop restaurant overlooking Los Angeles for a romantic evening, complete with a spectacular view of the city lights. Madonna wore a frilly purple skirt with a translucent white shirt and her characteristic black bra poking out from behind. They ate Japanese food at the restaurant and then left after three hours of what looked to some spectators to be minimal talk for a nightclub named Façade.

"I've been nibbling around the edges of this thing long enough, because I didn't know where to start or how to tell you," Prince said Madonna while they were out with pals at the club. He was being far braver than he'd ever been with her, and he was doing it in front of witnesses, which made it even more startling. "Madonna, I think you and I should hook up." "I want you to be my girl," I say.

Madonna, who appeared astonished, let the request linger, as if anticipating a punch line. He wasn't, however, joking. He waited for her reaction. "Hmmm," she responded, frowning and looking as if she was unsure how to handle the situation. "Now, that's food for thought, isn't it?" Her statements were lacking in conviction.

Madonna clasped Prince's hand when he appeared deflated. "C'mon, let's dance!" she exclaimed as she led him out onto the dance floor.

Madonna felt bored with Prince after around two months, when there was nothing left for them to say to one other. They'd recorded a few songs in his Minneapolis studio, one of which would be published later. But, according to her acquaintances, while she grumbled about his passivity, he moaned about her aggressive personality.

According to T. L. Ross, "Prince is a little too cosmic for Madonna." Making love is a spiritual experience for him. Making love was only a bodily expression for her, at least at the time. While he wanted to enjoy every moment of it, she was into several orgasms. He let her go after two months. She then performed the scorned lady act.

"When he stopped pretending to be interested in her, the phone calls began. Madonna had been bothering him for weeks. He subsequently said that she screamed at him, "How dare you dump me!" 'Do you have no idea who I am?' She was unaccustomed to being dumped."

Years later, in October 1994, Madonna would have the last word on

Prince, telling the Los Angeles Times, "I was having dinner with Prince and he was just sipping tea, very daintily." I was pushing food down my throat and thinking, 'Aren't you going to eat?' She faked a gentle nay and whispered it. She went on to say, "And I thought, 'Oh my God!'" I have a hypothesis about folks who refuse to eat. They irritate me."

8. "Madonna: A Lonely Life"

Following her brief romance with Prince, Madonna began to focus on Sean Penn as a possible mate. Despite her zealous demand for the spotlight and Sean Penn's obsessive need for solitude, the two embarked on a passionate and exhilarating courtship that demonstrated, if nothing else, that opposites do attract. Impressed by his tough guy reputation as well as his acting abilities, Madonna later admitted that she was "completely unable to resist him, not that I ever tried." He was the most attractive and intelligent man I had ever met." Sean was equally enthralled by her. He was a Madonna fan, which is why he wanted to meet her. Once he got to know her, he realised she was a lot of fun to be around and also the type of woman who would meet him at his level of arrogance when appropriate. "I'll admit it, I was a smart-ass," he admits. "She was as well. It was a match made in heaven, two smart-asses navigating life together. "How lovely."

At the time, with everyone attempting to get a piece of her — or so it must have felt to her — Madonna had stated that she wanted someone in her life who she believed truly loved her. "She was lonely, the classic victim of stardom in that she was the popular and well-loved celebrity who went home alone at night and cried her eyes out," her ex-producer and boyfriend Jellybean Benitez claimed. While she had plenty of sexual experiences, she lacked a genuine sense of closeness with another person. Of course, people in her inner circle at the time admit that Madonna was not an easy person to come to know or be emotionally connected with.

Sean Penn was not without insecurities. His obsession with privacy was obsessive, according to those who knew him well, and it sprang from the fact that he was never content with the way he looked, always feeling uneasy in his own skin and not wanting to be seen by anyone, let alone everyone. According to many who knew him well, his arrogance and bad temper were a camouflage that concealed a slew of other emotional disorders, the explanations of which are perhaps better left to Sean Penn biographers. When he and Madonna started dating, they discovered something in each other that gave them, as Madonna put it, "a sense of personal completion." Their sexual chemistry was also explosive. He flung her on the floor after their first date and pulled off her clothing and his own in such a haste that he left his boots on. After that, he made love to her. "We reached orgasm together," she later remarked, "and it was as if time stood still."

"Who's to say how the heart works... it just does," Meg Lowery, Sean's actress friend who lived in Los Angeles at the time and attended acting lessons with him, comments. "Sean told me he was madly in love with her. He was concerned, however. 'She's insane,' he said. 'And I'm insane. What about the two of us? That's a problem.' He also had a feeling she wouldn't be faithful to him. 'She's out there somewhere, wild and free,' he said. 'And I don't think any man can tame her. 'In fact,' he continued, 'I think the last thing she wants is to be tamed.'"

Sean Penn was a skilled actor and a bright man, in addition to his moody personality. Madonna was even more drawn to him when she discovered he was an avid reader and poet. Soon, she was telling everyone, friend or foe, that Sean Penn was her hero, best buddy, and the "coolest guy in the universe." She suggested she could tell him about her concerns. Despite the fact that both of his parents were still alive, he had the instinctual insight of a man who had suffered and knew everything there was to know about loss and sadness. She could communicate with him as she could with no one else.

The couple confirmed their engagement shortly after. As word of this major event circulated, interest in Madonna's life and career reached a new high. The men's magazine Penthouse stated that it will be publishing nude images of Madonna shot years previously, which surprised some of her followers but not those who knew her. Playboy, not to be outdone, promised the impending publication of similarly scandalous pictures. As a media phenomenon erupted around the possibility that images of Madonna would expose her in a new and revealing light, it was reminiscent of the revelation that Marilyn Monroe had likewise posed naked thirty-five years earlier.

Some commentators speculated that Madonna's naked images would harm her career. Reporters referred to Vanessa Williams, who had been compelled to return her Miss America crown a year before. It was discovered that she had posed naked years before winning her title. (Of course, Vanessa Williams would use the scandal to her advantage in the end. She is now one of the few Miss Americas whose name is even remembered.) The existence of nude photographs, the battle between two men's magazines to beat each other to publication, and Madonna's forthright remark, "I'm not ashamed of anything," only stoked the flames of a raging media fire.

Tommy Quinn had not seen Madonna in over a year when he received a phone call from her, he claims. She inquired as to whether they might meet. "No," she answered when he asked her to his residence. I'm now a caged animal. If I come to see you, everyone will know where you live and who I am, and they will never leave you alone." He goes on to say, "In order to protect me, she wanted us to meet in a small Italian restaurant on Second Avenue near Seventy-first Street."

When he arrived, Madonna was in a rear booth wearing enormous sunglasses, a floppy hat, and an old, worn flower-print "house dress." "She looked like a bag lady," he recalls. "I was astounded."

"What the hell happened to you?" he questioned, taking a seat.

"This is my life. That's exactly what happened to me," Madonna said glumly. She leaned in and kissed him on the cheek. "How do you think my outfit looks?" I'm a millionaire, yet I have to wear this in public just to have some peace and quiet."

Madonna got to the point of why she wanted to see her buddy after ordering spaghetti. "I need your advice," she explained. "Have you heard about these pictures?"

"Who hasn't?" Quinn responded.

She removed her sunglasses. She appeared to have been crying. "I just don't know how to deal with this goddamn thing," she admitted, her voice shaking. "I mean, I don't know how to be . . . how to act."

Years later, Quinn would recall, "I was taken aback. When I originally heard about the photos, I assumed she would say they didn't matter and that she was above worrying about them. But, as I sat with her, watching how upset she was, I realised that the existence of these images had genuinely bothered her."

"Oh, screw it, Madonna," Quinn said. "You must act as if you don't care. "Do you have a choice?"

"But I do care," she explained. "What about my dad?" Why should he have to look at those images? Sean, too! "How will Sean react?" Her fury flared. "Parasites!" she yelled at the media. "I feel so . . . misunderstood."[8]

Over two dishes of pasta with meatballs and a bottle of Merlot, Madonna reminisced about a time not so long ago, in 1979, when she decided to pose naked. "He was a nice guy, actually," she claimed of Martin Schreiber, the photographer. "At least, that's what I thought at the time." He made me feel good. He complimented my physique. In his loft studio, he wined and dined me. I had faith in him. And I guess I was an idiot for doing so."

Madonna and Tommy eventually agreed that she had no choice but to act as if the images didn't exist, just like Marilyn Monroe had done before her. The story of Marilyn Monroe's naked session in front of the camera is legendary in Hollywood. The images were revealed a few years after she posed, when she was possibly the most famous actress in the world. The sceptics in the press claimed that if the lovely young woman laid naked on red velvet was truly Marilyn Monroe, the controversy would undoubtedly end her career. Marilyn, unfazed by the media's hysteria, did not refute the images. Instead, she used the attention to her advantage, telling reporters, "Sure, I posed. "I was starving." When asked what she was listening to throughout the sessions, she joked, "the radio."

"If they [presumably the public and press] know I'm unhappy about them, they'll just love that," Madonna said, sounding dejected. "Oh, who cares anyway?" she continued, forcedly cheerful. "I have press agents now, you know?" she continued. "Let them sort it out on their own. I'll make use of this situation in some way. Do you realise that, Tommy?"

"Hell yeah, you will," Quinn said as she nudged her. "You're bigger than this, anyway, Madonna."

He recalls her forcing a mournful smile before making a mocking cross sign.

"Are you happy, Madonna?" he inquired. She didn't seem to mean to answer the question as she rose, hugged him, and said good-bye. She threw a fifty-dollar bill on the table. "Look at my life," she remarked, her brow furrowed. "Who wouldn't be happy?"

9. The Remake of Apocalypse Now

Sean Penn appears to have felt Madonna wanted "a nice, quiet ceremony," the site of which was to be kept a well guarded secret, despite the fact that such an idea contradicted everything everyone else thought they knew about the publicity-hungry diva. The invites, penned by her brother Michael and printed on hot pink paper, bore no address, location, or phone number. ("We cordially invite you to Sean and Madonna's birthday party. The festivities will begin at six o'clock. Please be there on time or you will miss their wedding." Those on the short list recognized that the bride would be twenty-seven on her wedding day, and the bridegroom would be twenty-five the next day.) Less than twenty-four hours before the ceremony, guests were to be told of the location via phone at their houses or hotels. The location of the event was only to be known to select staff at the caterer, chair rental company, and florist. The address was only to be revealed to delivery drivers once their trucks were loaded and ready to travel. Supervisors were also to follow the trucks to ensure that no driver stopped on his way to the ceremony to make a phone call that (for a few dollars) would tip off any press personnel as to what was going on and where.

Of course, word quickly spread that the Penn/Madonna wedding would take place on August 16, 1985, at six p.m., on the very visible Point Dume, Malibu, hilltop property of real estate tycoon Don Unger.

The pair had gotten married four days before. Sean Penn's middle name is "Justin," and he was born on August 17, 1960. At the time, he lived at 6728 Zumirez Road in Malibu. The highest school grade earned was a twelfth. His father's name was Leo Penn, and his mother's name was Eileen Annuci. Actor is my occupation.

Madonna used the same address as Sean at the time because they were living together. Her job title is "entertainer."

There was a lot of squabbling in the days leading up to the wedding around Sean's refusal to sign a prenuptial agreement. Madonna's advisors were adamant that she not marry without first having a "prenup" with her fiancé in place, and they badgered her until she ultimately — and, one could infer, reluctantly — persuaded Sean to sign one. He was adamant that he would never do anything like that. "I equated it to a death warrant in a marriage," he subsequently explained. Perhaps he was aware that the request was coming from attorneys and managers (who he later described as "a bunch of pathetic idiots who were accusing me of trying to cash in, move in on Madonna's money"). It was utterly absurd, and it truly irritated me.") Sean had to have been worried about what would happen to him as Madonna's husband. "She had become a one-person megacompany," he explained, "and all of those people were on the phone with her every day, making sure I wasn't looking for money, as if I didn't have my own career." "You chumps."

"Look, Sean, just sign the goddamn papers," Madonna instructed him in front of one of her lawyers.

"Fuck you, Madonna," he replied angrily. "I ain't singing nothing."

"Then I'm not marrying you," she said.

"Fine," he replied. "Fuck you, anyway."

"No," she replied. "Fuck you, Sean."

"No," he replied. "Fuck you, Madonna."

And so it went...

After all of the yelling and screaming, Sean did not sign a prenuptial agreement. The wedding plans were finalised, despite the fact that several observers thought these two people hardly liked, let alone loved, each other. There was little affection between them. Sean was distant, and Madonna was cold. They seemed to irritate each other.

Still, the marriage went ahead. Perhaps in their quiet moments alone, away from the public spotlight, they shared something no one else knew about, something they understood as genuine love and trust: a foundation for a life together.

Despite the "precautions," there was simply no way to ensure that the word of this marriage ceremony would not be leaked. Some of Madonna's friends joked that she probably snuck into a hotel room and called the National Enquirer herself. In less than an hour, it appeared that nearly every tabloid reporter in the Los Angeles area — more than a hundred of them in any case — had gathered in front of Unger's $6.5-million mansion, plotting ways to get a closer look, paying caterers to gain access. Media outfits began making arrangements with people to rent adjoining houses in order to utilise cameras with telephoto lenses for exclusive images.

The wedding ceremony, which featured a celebrity-driven guest list of over 200 people (including Andy Warhol, Tom Cruise, David Letterman, and Cher), was a highly publicised flop. The property was not just encircled by press, but photographers were also suspended from the trees. Earlier, Sean had attempted to persuade Madonna to allow the press to take a few brief shots in private in order to relieve some of the tension surrounding the occasion, but Madonna refused such a "photo op."

Initially, the helicopters hovered 500 feet over the wedding. They came dangerously close to the ground as soon as Madonna walked out of the house, whipping the hair of the female visitors with the might of their whirling blades. Sean Penn cursed as he sprinted around the perimeter of the seaside home, firing at the eight helicopters circling above. Madonna appeared surprised. The open disdain imprinted on her groom's cruel face had to have been shocking. "I would have been very excited to see one of those helicopters burn and the bodies inside melt," he said at the time. "They didn't seem like people to me. I've never fired a gun at anything I perceived to be a living being."

"I realised then," Madonna would later recall, "that my life would never be the same."

Madonna looked lovely in a strapless, white (!) $10,000 wedding gown (designed by her "Like a Virgin" tour designer, Marlene Stewart), walking down the aisle on the arm of her father, Tony. Madonna was wearing a black-rimmed hat under her veil, which she had to pull down to keep it from flying away. Her hair was twisted into a French twist beneath the cap. Sean was dressed in a $695 double-breasted Gianni Versace suit. His tie was knotted haphazardly. While shaving, he had missed a few places.

Female guests began screaming as Madonna clenched her fists fiercely at the helicopters, their long gowns flying up. "Welcome to the remaking of Apocalypse Now," Sean Penn welcomed the windswept audience. The bride and groom then began yelling their vows to Malibu judge John Merrik above the din. In the middle of "I do take you," Madonna raised her middle finger. Sean's face looked sombre during the service.

The five-minute ceremony included the pair exchanging basic gold rings. Penn then lifted his wife's veil and kissed her to the accompaniment of Chariots of Fire while the guests stood and applauded. Following that, on a balcony a few feet above the visitors, Sean toast "the most beautiful woman in the world." Then he was supposed to take off his wife's $700 custom-made garter. Madonna raised her gown delicately so Sean could discover it. But, just as indelicately, Sean vanished beneath the billowing skirts, where he seemed to be crawling around and struggling to find the garter. He eventually found it. Madonna tossed it into the throng, where it was recovered by her sister Paula, who was also her maid of honour. The wedding dinner — lobster in a white cream sauce, swordfish, and a mixed vegetable side dish — was then held under a large tent on the front lawn of the home (of course!), catered by Los Angeles chef (and owner of the famous Spago restaurant) Wolfgang Puck. Three fully stocked bars, each eight feet long, took the visitors' attention away from the circling helicopters. No live band performed during the wedding reception, much to the surprise of some guests, including Cher, who exclaimed, "What? Could she not afford live entertainment? We must listen to records? At home, I could listen to records! And without the use of helicopters!"

Madonna danced with the guests during the reception to Prince and Michael Jackson songs. Meanwhile, Sean appeared gloomy and dejected, just like he had at his bachelor celebration.

Later, behaving glumly, Madonna referred to the wedding as a "circus," as if this were a bad thing - something she hadn't anticipated. "Damn them," she said to one of her associates about the press's intrusion. "Damn them all to hell for ruining my special day."

"Really?" the associate inquired. "You didn't expect all of this to happen?"

"I didn't say that," Madonna humbly said. "But damn them, anyway," she said, smiling. (Later, in a Saturday Night Live sketch, she mocked the ceremony, indicating either her sense of humour about it or the fact that she wasn't all that angry about how it ended out.)

Madonna, in fact, had arranged the ultimate press event. "What better way to appear on the cover of Time?" And Life, and People. "And every other magazine," Martin Ciccone, Madonna's brother, remarked. "Everything was calculated. Without a doubt, she is a marketing genius."

"I thought it was a lovely affair," her father, Tony, remarked fifteen years later. Perhaps only a father could look past the squabbles to see his daughter, dressed in white, marrying the man of her dreams. He recalls Madonna asking him, "Are you proud of me, Daddy?" soon before she married Sean.

"I have always been proud of you," he said.

"Daddy, that's not true," she countered. "Just be honest with me, for once."

"But why won't you just believe that I am proud of you," she said to him.

Tony would later recollect Madonna crying as she said, "Because you never wanted any of this for me." You didn't want me to be a dancer, much less what I became. You simply desired that I stay at home, attend college, marry, and have children."

Tony struggled to understand the significance of his daughter's words. While he had urged her to go to college, he had never shown her as much disinterest in her profession as she had frequently claimed. It was evident that something else was wrong, that Madonna was angry with him about something else. Because father and daughter had never properly spoken their emotions in an honest, direct manner, the true basis of Madonna's bitterness toward Tony would have to go untreated.

"Well, you're getting married now, aren't you?" Tony Ciccone came to an end. "That's gotta count for something, doesn't it?"

10. Trouble in "Paradise"

By mid-1986, Madonna's musical career had reached new heights; she couldn't have been more pleased with the achievements of her True Blue venture, both artistically and commercially. Her personal life, on the other hand, was less than ideal; her marriage had gone deeper into disrepair. The pair appeared to disagree on everything, even her unwillingness to be tested for the HIV virus. At the time, little was known about HIV, and there was significant debate regarding the benefits and drawbacks of being tested for it. Today, Madonna, an AIDS fighter, would almost likely advise that a sexually active individual be tested for the HIV virus on a regular basis. However, she appeared to be just as perplexed as the rest of the populace about the hazards of fatal HIV.

Sean Penn paused to admire his wife's odd outfit, maybe admiring her beauty, elusiveness, and flawless style. She looked at him as well. Madonna snapped her fingers twice without looking away from him. A subordinate approached her and placed a freshly lit cigarette between her lips. She puffed away. Sean smiled. "That's my wife," he answered, tolerantly dismissing the pointless debate.

"Oh, screw you, Sean," Madonna murmured from the corner of her mouth.

"Yeah, well," he murmured, "not until you get tested."

In the summer of 1986, Madonna's good friend and former roommate in New York, artist Martin Burgoyne, was diagnosed with AIDS. Madonna was distraught. Earlier, Sean had flown Martin and Erica Bell out to Malibu from New York for a party to celebrate the release of "Papa Don't Preach." Madonna quickly recognized Burgoyne was ill. He called her a few weeks later to inform her of the awful news.

As a last-ditch effort to save Burgoyne, Madonna requested Sean to fly to Mexico and purchase an experimental treatment that was not available in the United States. She believed the medicine would "cure" her pal. Of course, it didn't. Martin died in November 1986, shortly before Thanksgiving, when he was only twenty-three years old. Madonna kept his hand at his deathbed until he died. She paid $4,000 for his memorial service.

Sean did everything he could to console Madonna following Martin's death, displaying a compassionate, sympathetic side. His all-too-frequent jealous outbursts, on the other hand, had become a big issue.

One of the earliest indications that Sean's often violent attitude may be aimed not only toward photographers but even toward his own wife came before their wedding, when he discovered she had once dated Prince. Sean punched a hole through the wall after a dispute about the rock star. Madonna has later stated that she was stunned and terrified by the occurrence. "That's when I first saw the appearance of the demon," she went on to say. "I should have known then that there would be trouble."

Madonna narrated the story as if she were narrating the scenario of a thrilling soap drama on television. "Oh, my God, Melinda," she exclaimed. "Sean found out about me and Prince, and we had this incredible fight." I told him to fuck off and that I could do anything I wanted. He was so enraged that he stormed out the door, and I slammed it shut behind him. "Then he came back in," she continued, hurriedly, "and I swear to Christ, Melinda, he was so mad at me, he punched this hole in the wall." Take a look at that. Is that cool or what?"

"That's cool?" Melinda inquired, her gaze drawn to the hole. "That is not cool, Madonna. That's frightening."

"What are you talking about?" Madonna was ecstatic. "I mean, how much must he love me, to punch a hole in the wall like that." (A few days later, Madonna called Prince and asked him to come to her house and mend the hole, "because you're responsible for it, after all." As directed, Prince arrived with plaster and repaired the hole.)

Now that they are married, Madonna didn't think Sean's aggressive tendency was so "cool." When he was agitated, he would grab one of his guns and fire a string of shots at rabbits or birds. He strolled around the house with a loaded gun tucked into the back of his pants, which appeared to Madonna's concerned friends, if not to the lady herself, to be a sort of emotional abuse.

Sean's close friend describes what transpired during a dinner gathering at the Penns' house. "We were at the pool. Sean had a little too much to drink. Madonna did, too. There was a guy there who had been staring at her all night. Madonna walked over to him and began flirting with him."

"What's this all about?" Sean remarked harshly as he moved over to them.

"Oh, get lost, Sean," Madonna said. "We're just talking."

Sean grabbed up his wife and hurled her into the pool without hesitation. The throng of roughly thirty people appeared to be in shock. Madonna swam leisurely to the shallow end of the pool and then ascended its few stairs as they looked on. She strolled across the terrace and into the house, dripping wet and silent. "She never came back out," a buddy recalls.

Earlier that year, Madonna and Penn were dining at Helena's, one of their favourite Los Angeles restaurants, when an old friend, David Wolinsky (from the group Rufus, which included Chaka Khan), approached her at their table, stooped over, and gave her an innocent kiss in greeting. Penn jumped out of his chair and attacked Wolinsky, hitting and kicking him. Only when stunned bystanders were able to detain Penn did the attack come to an end. Madonna was humiliated.

"She looked like she wanted to crawl into a hole," one witness said. "I remember watching her as she glared at Sean and thinking to myself, she's starting to hate him."

Sean Penn had recovered from the Shanghai Surprise disaster and was working on a gritty cop drama, Colors, with Dennis Hopper. Meanwhile, Madonna was exploring numerous scripts for herself. She was eager to duplicate Judy Holliday's big 1950 comedy Born Yesterday or Marlene Dietrich's star-making role in the 1929 drama The Blue Angel, influenced by her love of old Hollywood. In terms of fresh screenplays, she was offered Blind Date and an early version of Evita (which would remain in production for years). She was, however, most keen to appear in a Carole Lombard screwball comedy. Slammer was about a crazy blonde named Nikki Finn (Madonna) who, after being released from jail for a crime she did not commit, sets out to find the man who framed her. The typical screwball issues arise, including chase sequences, mobsters, and a 160-pound cougar. An agreement was struck, and filming in New York commenced. Perhaps because Sean was now awaiting sentencing on the assault charges, the title of the film was changed from Slammer (which, her handlers reasoned, was where Penn was heading) to Who's That Girl?

Meanwhile, in Los Angeles, Sean's violent temper got him into problems again when he attacked a thirty-two-year-old actor on the set of Colors. Sean emerged from nowhere as the young extra knelt on the sidelines with a camera, looking for a good shot. He snatched the camera from the extra's grasp. "You bastard," Sean said with a snort, "don't take any pictures of me between takes." Then he punched him in the face.

11. Who's That Girl?

Although Madonna actively promoted the film, posing for many magazine covers in the style of Marilyn Monroe, Who's That Girl? would go on to become another box-office flop, no doubt because its star was attempting to be so many different things she wasn't. By borrowing a Judy Holliday voice, as well as Marilyn Monroe's hair and makeup, for a film that looked tailor-made for Carole Lombard, Madonna demonstrated that she was not up to the task at hand. Variety dubbed the film "a rattling failure," and the majority of other critics agreed.

So far on the big screen, Madonna had been most successful in Desperately Seeking Susan, a film in which she played herself and exploited many of her own personal attributes. If she had continued to brand her performances with her own distinct and, by this point, easily identifiable identity (at least until she was more proficient at constructing characters), her film career could have taken off in the same manner that her singing career did. However, Madonna came across as unnecessarily cloying in her attempt to build a popular character for Who's That Girl? by mimicking her movie idols rather than using her own personality. "I don't like that movie," she stated in February 2000. "I'm not happy with my performance in it." I'd argue there are some decent parts in any other movie I've made. Or I believe my performance was good, but the film was not. What's the name of that girl? "I think it was all pretty bad."

If Madonna was anxious that the film's failure would mark the end of her career, she was mistaken. After all, she still had her incredible recording career.

As far as soundtracks go, Who's That Girl? was a collection of nine songs from the film rather than a traditional one. While Madonna only featured four tracks on the album, each was significant since it indicated the record might potentially sell on the strength of her appearance alone. Madonna, who was twenty-nine at the time, was not only one of the hottest singers in popular music, but also one with evident and tremendous staying power. Who's That Girl? was a low-budget film with a cast of performers who weren't likely to win Oscars anytime soon, so the soundtrack was just as crucial to Warner Bros. Records as the film itself.

When Madonna was given the task of writing and producing the film's title song, she teamed up with her co-writers/producers, Steve Bray and Patrick Leonard, and set to work. Other tracks on the album were primarily provided by obscure Warner Bros. Records performers including Club Nouveau, Michael Davidson, and Scritti Politti.

Madonna, of course, was responsible for keeping the Who's That Girl? soundtrack out of record store discount bins. The title track and first single, written and produced by Madonna and Leonard, were characteristic Madonna music: funky, sassy, and lyrical, with a Latin twist. It quickly rose to the top of the Billboard singles charts.

The soundtrack's second song, Bray's party groove,""Causing a Commotion," achieved exactly that on both worldwide dance floors and the US singles chart, reaching number two. The other two Madonna tracks — "The Look of Love," an exotic Madonna/Leonard ballad, and "Can't Stop," an uptempo Madonna/Bray composition — were purposefully left on the soundtrack album to encourage LP sales. It was successful. The album Who's That Girl? sold over a million copies in the United States and five million worldwide.

Riding on Madonna's coattails proved profitable for everyone involved, including Warner Bros. Records, which made big sales with a compilation that was essentially a showcase for its marginal artists; the artists and producers themselves, most of whom had never been involved in a project as successful, before or since; and Peter Guber and Jon Peters, the film's producers, for whom the album's brisk sales served as the bright spot in a film enterprise whose overall success was mediocre.

Meanwhile, the world first witnessed Madonna's new updated, sleek image in concert during 1987's "Who's That Girl?" tour - a look devoid of bangles, jewellery, and other embellishments.

Madonna's "Who's That Girl?" tour was musically and technically superior to her first concert appearances in that she included multimedia elements to make the show even more interesting.

Her dancers were also instructed not to address her, a far cry from the bond she would subsequently create with her ensemble on the "Blonde Ambition" tour. Unless they were onstage with her, her musicians were not even allowed to glance at her. Furthermore, upon entering and exiting the stage, Madonna insisted that road managers place sheets around her to screen her from the gaze of those who couldn't help but stare because, after all, she was Madonna. Her dressing area had to be redecorated to her specifications at each point along the route, with new carpeting, fresh paint (always pink), new furniture... and so much Mexican cuisine that it would have taken an army to eat it all. "She has a way of demanding that compels you to give her your undivided attention," explains Freddy DeMann.

Melinda Cooper, Freddy DeMann's assistant, received a phone call from Madonna one evening at a very late hour. She was waiting for a limousine to take her to a party, but it hadn't arrived yet.

"The goddamn car isn't here yet," Madonna yelled. "It's, like, fifteen minutes late, Melinda."

"It'll be there soon," Melinda recalls patiently saying.

"Why, you idiot," Madonna yelled at her over the phone. "It is your responsibility, Melinda, to ensure that the limousine arrives on time. "Do you know how much work I have?" she questioned, her temper flaring. "I've got a lot on my plate, Melinda, and all you have to do is get the car here on time." And can you pull it off? No, you can't. "What's the matter with you, Melinda?"

"But, Madonna..." Melinda started.

"Don't 'But, Madonna,'" she murmured, cutting her off. "Look, here's the deal: if the fucking car isn't here in five minutes, you're finished."

Madonna hung up the phone.

Melinda Cooper broke down in tears.

12. Dinner with Warren

Despite her incredible success as a recording artist, Madonna aspired to be recognized as a film actor. She must have realised that her Broadway experience had done little to increase her marketability as a Hollywood actor. Typically, she kept her sights set on her goal and directed her film agents to continue looking for properties in which she could star and roles for which she may be a good fit. In the fall of 1988, she was offered a part in a picture she felt she couldn't pass up, a new Warren Beatty feature that was in the works. The picture, Dick Tracy, was based on the popular comic strip character and had all the makings of a blockbuster, something Madonna desired in her career as badly as she desired anything at this moment in her life. Breathless Mahoney, the gorgeous femme fatale, seemed tailor-made for her.

The issue was that the calibre of Madonna's previous movie work did little to entice Beatty to cast her opposite him as the film's Mahoney. Kathleen Turner, whose sensuous voice had brought erotic layers to the character of Jessica Rabbit in Who Framed Roger Rabbit?, was his favourite. Beatty thought the beautiful Kim Basinger, who had been smashing in a comparable fantasy film, Batman, could add the same type of sexual shine to the female lead in Dick Tracy.

Warren Beatty wanted to meet with Madonna to discuss the film, but she declined. "It took me weeks to get a date with her," he said once.

Madonna emphasised in her book Sex, published in the 1990s, that "the best way to seduce someone is to make yourself unavailable." All you have to do is be busy all the time, and they'll be begging to see you. Then, for the first five dates, you don't fuck them. Allow them to come closer and closer, but don't fuck them."

When Madonna agreed to let Warren take her out to dinner at Los Angeles' Ivy restaurant, she finally turned on the charm to persuade him to cast her in the part. She asked a lot of questions while wearing a sleek, black leather jumpsuit that was unzipped in a revealing manner and a matching leather helmet. She was definitely attempting to learn more about him, his flaws, and anything else that could be useful. He followed suit. Madonna added to Beatty later, "I know you've heard a lot of terrible things about me, and I'm here to tell you that they're all true." She burst out laughing. "How about you?" she inquired. "I've heard great things about you. True?" Warren remained silent. "Exactly as I predicted," Madonna stated. "All true."

Warren later stated that Madonna's sense of humour immediately hit him. She was charming and seductive, and she was ideal for the part for which she was auditioning. After dropping her off, he kissed her on the doorstep. "Houston," he is claimed to have declared after kissing her, "we have lift-off."

"He thought she was pretty great," Beatty's pal stated. "He hired her on the spot."

The truth is that Kathleen Turner and Kim Basinger were both unavailable at the time. Beatty might have kept seeking for his Breathless Mahoney or hired Madonna. He plainly didn't think she was worth much as an actress, because he requested her to audition for the part for Screen Actors Guild scale wages of only $1,440 per week. So, in effect, Madonna's involvement significantly reduced the film's budget because neither Turner nor Bassinger would ever work in a $60-million budget film for less than $2,000 per week — nor would any popular actress, unless she was wise enough to recognize that such a decision could be a brilliant career move. After all, Dick Tracy offered high production values and an all-star cast that included Al Pacino, Gene Hackman, and Mandy Patinkin, as well as cameos by Dick van Dyke, James Caan, and Charles Durning. As a big summer movie from Disney, it was practically sure to do well. Madonna knew that if the film fell by chance, it couldn't be placed on her because she was only one star in an ensemble piece. If it is a success, she will be credited with her first screen bonanza, and she will be able to exploit it to demonstrate her box-office appeal. In addition, Madonna's contract stated that she would earn a percentage of the film's profits in exchange for her minimal fee. As a result, Dick Tracy created a win-win situation for Madonna. She was astute enough to perceive it that way and enthusiastically accepted a deal that several in the business saw as an insult, especially given her position in the entertainment industry.

13. Malibu Nightmare

Madonna's marriage to Sean Penn had been together for more than three years by Christmas 1988. To say the forty months since their union on August 16, 1985, had been tough would be an understatement of epic proportions. Penn's drinking and violent temper were too much for Madonna, and by the end of 1988, the marriage was all but finished. She described it as if she had married a toddler in a man's body, someone with the emotional capacity of a ten-year-old.

Of course, by this point, Madonna had realised that Sean Penn had a drinking problem, which made it impossible for him to focus on mending their marriage. His temper was more volatile than ever. For example, after a particularly heated dispute, he threatened to drown their dog, Hank. Madonna managed to persuade him to reconsider. The next day, at the recommendation of actor Robert Duvall, she drove Sean to Palm Springs to the Betty Ford Center, hoping to persuade him to dry out. They signed in as Mr. and Mrs. Victor Cobb, but after discussing with counsellors, they recognized they had a slim chance of keeping Sean's presence hidden from the press. They weren't even halfway back to Los Angeles on the two-hour drive home when calls from Madonna's manager Freddy DeMann began flooding in on their vehicle phone, informing them that they had been spotted at the Betty Ford Center. "But how did anyone know?" Madonna recalls asking Freddy. "Someone must have told someone."

"The press is psychic when it comes to you," he said to her.

Madonna was at a loss for what to do with Sean once she returned to Malibu. "I know I have to help him. "But he doesn't want any help," Sandra Bernhard subsequently recalled. Sandra had travelled to the West Coast to spend Thanksgiving with Madonna.

"I don't know what to do," Madonna added. "His drinking is causing havoc in our marriage." He shoves me away. "I'm depressed."

"Let me ask you a simple question," Sandra said. "Do you ever have fun?"

"What do you mean?"

"Have some fun, Madonna. "Do you and Sean ever have a good time?"

Madonna appeared depressed. She had answered her friend's query without saying anything.

"Then he's got to go," Sandra said.

Madonna consented, despite the fact that she and Sean had discussed having a child to save their marriage. She'd assured him that 1989 would be the year they'd start a family. She was afraid of having Sean's child because she didn't want a child to grow up in a damaged home, "and we are nothing if not broken," she added bitterly.

"You're insane to bring a child into this mess," Sandra replied. "I'm telling you, he's got to go."

Madonna asked Sean to leave after another fight. He relocated to live with his father, filmmaker Leo Penn. A few days later, on December 26, Sean called Madonna to discuss the status of their relationship. Madonna informed Sean during the conversation that she had decided not to have his child. She stated that by signing a deal to star in Dick Tracy, she would have to postpone having a family for another year.

According to paperwork Madonna later filed with the Los Angeles County CourtHouse, Penn was "disgusted and pissed off" with her after that chat, and they got into a heated dispute.

"It's over," Madonna remembers telling Sean over the phone. "I'm looking for a divorce." "I require a divorce."

She must have been trembling as she hung up the phone.

Madonna called John F. Kennedy in New York that afternoon. Recalls Mr. Stephen Styles, "By this point, John and Madonna's romance had cooled, but she still relied on him for emotional support." She asked him to fly to the West Coast and assist her with some marital troubles." Styles claims Madonna told Kennedy that she needed "moral support to get through this time in my life."

John decided against flying to California. "I think he didn't want Madonna depending on him," Stephen Styles speculated. "He was afraid that if he came to her rescue every time she called, they'd get back together — which would only upset his mother, and he didn't want to do that." He felt awful about it, but he also didn't want to drop everything and be at Madonna's disposal.

"Instead, what he did was track down Sean," Stephen Styles adds. "He knew his phone number. Madonna had earlier given it to him. And John called Sean and said, 'If you lay one hand on her, I will come out there and pulverise you, you little punk.' He even threatened him with physical assault. Penn was enraged and threatened to call the cops on him. As a result, John took a step back. He didn't require that kind of attention."

Although the public saw Madonna as strong and independent, she was genuinely scared and weak at the time, leading some of her friends to question what was going on in her marriage. Sean Penn was undoubtedly irritated that Madonna appeared to be having an illicit affair with Warren Beatty. "He would follow her at night and they would always end up at Warren's," claims a Penn acquaintance. "He'd park in front of Beatty's gate and wait for her to leave." She would frequently refuse to do so until the sun rose. This, along with her decision not to start a family with him, was driving Sean insane. It was all building up in him, an anger that would erupt."

Madonna's telephonic proclamation of independence from her spouse on that December morning was the first step in reclaiming her identity. But it wasn't that simple. Nothing was ever straightforward with Sean.

Sean Penn allegedly scaled the wall around the Malibu property in the late afternoon of December 28, 1988, and rushed in, discovering Madonna alone in the master bedroom. She'd given the live-in help the night off so she could attend a holiday party. According to a police report Madonna later filed with the Malibu Sheriff's Office, the two began to argue again over Madonna's intention to divorce. When she told him she was leaving the house, he tried to bind her hands with an electric lamp and cord, according to the official investigation. Madonna bolted from her room.

Sean pursued her through the living room. According to the report, while there, he tied her to an easy chair with strong twine. Many other heinous things happened, at least according to published versions of the incident, none of which Madonna ever denied, but suffice it to say, it appears to have been a night of physical and emotional torture.

Penn was "drinking liquor straight from the bottle," according to the police report, and his abuse of her lasted many hours, during which time he allegedly smacked her and roughed her up. Penn went out to get more alcohol after a few hours. He returned some hours later and, according to the police report, continued his assaults on her.

According to government documents, Madonna finally convinced Sean to untie her by telling him she needed to go to the bathroom. She bolted from the house once she was free. Sean slipped while rushing after her, giving her an advantage. She climbed into the coral-coloured 1957 Thunderbird that Penn had given her for her 28th birthday. She had locked herself inside the vehicle.

While Sean hammered furiously on the car windows, Madonna dialled 911 on her cell phone. When she finished conversing with them, she shifted into reverse and drove away, heading for the Malibu Sheriff's Office on Pacific Coast Highway.

"When Madonna staggered into the station [fifteen minutes later], she was distraught, crying, and with makeup smeared all over her face," Lieutenant Bill McSweeney remembered. "I couldn't place her as Madonna, the singer." She was sobbing, her lip was bleeding, and she was bruised. She had clearly been struck. Without a question, this was a woman in serious difficulty."

Officers rushed to arrest Madonna's husband after being astonished by the information she had told about her nine-hour ordeal. Sean Penn was still inside the residence when the officers arrived. "We had to use our bullhorns," one cop recalled. 'Come out of the house, Sean Penn, with your hands in the air,' we said. "The suspect came out, and we handcuffed him."

14. Divorce

In most cases of domestic abuse, there are two sides to the tale. Madonna accused Penn of inflicting "corporal injury and traumatic conditions" on her as well as committing "battery." Sean Penn, on the other hand, has a different take on what happened in Malibu on that December day in 1988. He claims he never tied up his wife. He recalls that after a normal disagreement with him, Madonna stormed out of the house to cool off. He yelled after her that if she dared to return, he would cut off all of her hair. He claims that as a result of his warning, "she developed a fear of getting a very severe haircut." If Sean's allegation is true, it's reasonable that the thought of her enraged spouse coming at her with a pair of scissors would be horrifying to Madonna. "So, she took this concern to the local authorities, who came back up to the house," Sean went on to explain. "She felt the responsible thing would be to inform them — since they were coming up there ostensibly to keep her from getting a haircut and to let her gather some additional personal effects — that there were firearms in the house." He admits to having guns in his home. Sean was in the kitchen eating Rice Krispies cereal when the cops arrived, carrying bullhorns and handcuffs. Sean claims that the cops "suggested I come out of the house" because they were concerned he had a gun. They did what they had to do, the way they had to do it. That didn't bother me."

On the same day she filed for divorce, Madonna visited with Deputy District Attorney Lauren Weiss to inform her that she had decided to drop the charges against her husband. She was supposed to be afraid of the notoriety that a trial would undoubtedly bring. However, the truth is that she couldn't take the thought of Sean being tried. Despite how terribly their relationship had deteriorated, she still considered him to be the love of her life. She cared about him and wanted him to be secure. "May God bless and keep him," she stated at the time, "but far, far away from me." This marriage is over."

The manner in which Madonna's marriage ended would affect key facets of her personality. She'd become accustomed to having complete control over her life and her men. She took joy in it, even boasted about it. She displayed a stunning lack of sympathy at times and mocked women who appeared weak or sensitive as a result of a failed relationship. She never understood how a woman could let a man get the better of her. But Sean Penn put an end to her sense of control, and not just metaphorically.

The Malibu horror damaged Madonna in ways that only she can completely explain... and she hasn't seen fit to do so. Friends say she would have nightmares about that dreadful time in December when her husband lost control of his senses for the next few months. She appeared to be psychologically scarred by the incident, more so than she would admit to anybody other than close friends.

"She would start crying for no reason," a friend of hers who sought anonymity said. "At the time, I sensed she was depressed and lonely." Her supporters and the press portrayed her as powerful and self-sufficient, which she had been — and would continue to be. But her ordeal with Sean had left her emotionally scarred. As a result, she lost a lot of self-confidence and self-esteem, and it would take her years to recover. In some ways, I believe she still hasn't."

Madonna left her gold wedding ring on the bathroom vanity as she packed her things and left the Malibu home she and Sean had shared for her apartment in New York. It said, "M LOVES S."

Neither Madonna nor Sean would ever talk publicly about the incident. "Suffice it to say, Sean has a serious anger management problem," Madonna said in a pal. The fact that Madonna did not disclose the incident with the media tells a lot about her discomfort with what had happened. She'd certainly been known to go to the press with several events involving her personal life in the past... but not this one. According to some close to her, Madonna chose silence since she didn't know what to make of Sean's behaviour and couldn't stand discussing them. Furthermore, she didn't want to tarnish Sean's name in any way. After all, Madonna knew Sean better than most people, and she must have known that what happened in Malibu was not his greatest hour. She didn't want to tarnish his image by revealing what had happened between them.

Sean, for his part, was supposed to be grateful for Madonna's silence. He felt terrible, he told one friend, explaining that whiskey had led him into a serious error of judgement.

Sean didn't want any of Madonna's money, despite the fact that under California law, he was entitled to half of her fortune. Instead, he wanted Madonna to keep the entire $70 million her career had garnered for her in the three years she had been married. "I could have gone any way I wanted," he subsequently said. "In California, there is community property. But I would never, under any circumstances, take a dime from someone else's change."

Instead, Sean Penn walked away from the marriage with the nearly $5 million he had earned (despite being paid $1 million per film) as well as the couple's $2-million, three-bedroom, Spanish-style mansion. Penn profited $1.2 million on the joint property despite the fact that his personal investment was only $880,000. He also got to keep the home's Southwestern and Santa Fe-style furniture, including a log-built four-poster bed. Madonna removed all of the art deco and art nouveau paintings and sculptures. She did, however, leave behind a mangled doll with pins through it, according to one court document. Madonna kept their New York apartment, but gave Penn $498,000 — the value of his stake in that property. (She spent $2.9 million on a seven-bedroom mansion in the Hollywood Hills for herself.) According to court documents, she also turned over $18,700 in "short-term paper" investments and another $2,300 in cash (both from a shared financial account).

The divorce was formalised on January 25, 1989. Because the relevant documents had been prepared and then filed away so many times in the past, they were updated and available for Sean Penn to sign within days. Madonna had loved Sean and sincerely wanted to follow her marriage vows, thus the divorce devastated her. She hadn't been happy in a long time, so she might have imagined she wouldn't miss Sean. She was incorrect. She would later admit that she was astonished by the sense of loss she felt in the months following the final decision. On a deep level, as she would explain to others, she and Sean were "soul mates." It was difficult for her to comprehend how everything had turned out for them.

Today, people closest to her say she regrets her marriage to Sean. She can't help but romanticise her marriage to him, viewing it through a lens that obscures the darker sides of the relationship. To her credit, she only seems to want to remember good days with Sean — not the Malibu nightmare. Of course, some of her friends have asked when those joyful occasions occurred because most people never saw her and Sean being happy, at least not after their wedding ceremony — and Sean didn't appear very thrilled that day, either. However, no one knows what happens in a marriage when two individuals are alone except the two persons involved.

Madonna also believes, or has acknowledged privately, that she could have been more forgiving of Sean's views regarding Sandra Bernhard. She also wonders if she should have been more proactive in getting him to stop drinking. She admitted to feeling guilty because "I should have made him stop." Every time we drank a drink together, I felt bad about it."

Her Catholic background may have contributed to part of her guilt. "Once you're a Catholic, you're always a Catholic — in terms of your feelings of guilt and remorse and whether you've sinned or not," she said in a telephone interview. "Sometimes I feel guilty when I don't need to be, and I attribute this to my Catholic upbringing." Because under Catholicism, you are born a sinner and remain a sinner throughout your life. The sin is always within you, no matter how hard you strive to avoid it."

Actually, Madonna could have done nothing to help the terribly defective Sean Penn. The truth appears to be that Penn was a coward. He wanted to break up with Madonna and stop their relationship for whatever reason, but lacked the strength to do so. Instead, he staged a horrifying situation that he knew would force her hand and force her to petition for divorce. "You can't change a person, or control their demons," Madonna subsequently stated of Sean Penn. "That's one of the things I learned from that relationship."

It may be argued that Sean and Madonna did their best with what they had in terms of common sense and maturity. The fact that they were both famous at such a young age didn't help their marriage either. Certainly, Madonna would never be as publicly hostile to her spouse as she was to Sean today. While she is still a complicated, volatile, and often difficult to comprehend person, she is clearly not the same woman she was a decade ago.

Madonna later admitted that her separation with Sean had left her "more suspicious of people." "You imbue men with the qualities you desire," she noticed. "Then they're not at all what you'd expect. But it's also your fault for not doing your homework and investigating. I've become more careful. "However, I'm still a hopeless romantic."

Sean Penn has worked hard to clean up his act since his marriage to Madonna - he's not "sober," but he hasn't been drunk in public in years. He has gone on to be a happy and productive person, yet some say he is still not the ideal mate. Since their marriage in 1996, he and his second wife, actress Robin Wright, mother of his two children, have had their own problems.

When asked if he thinks Madonna's marriage might have worked, he says, "No fucking way." Not with what we were up against." Reporters frequently seek Sean's opinion on the newest public relations sensation created by his ex-wife, believing him to be an authority on the matter. He usually has no opinion on anything. "Look, I'm not any better an expert on her than anyone else," he said. "Being with her hasn't made me know her any better. "I was drunk most of the time."

He and Madonna would continue to have intense feelings for each other for years to come, albeit they would rarely talk to each other. "It's too painful," Madonna said to writer Kevin Sessums when asked if she and Penn were still in contact. "It's horrible," she remarked, her eyes welling up with tears.

Years later, in 1995, while Madonna was accepting a VH1 Fashion and Music Award, Sean abruptly appeared on stage in front of a surprised audience. While Madonna revelled in startling others but rarely, if ever, revelled in it when the tables were reversed, she appeared genuinely pleased to see Sean. The two exchanged tender embraces. She stepped to the microphone after he left the stage and stated to the audience, "Now, that was really dirty."

Perhaps Madonna's brief reconnection with Sean Penn in 1995 reawakened something in her that had been dormant for some time. The next day, she wore a leopard-skin coat and tucked her hair under a hat before meeting the low-key, baseball-cap-wearing Penn in Central Park. "I miss you so much, baby," she was heard telling him. "Don't you miss me, too?" The always-present and agitated paparazzi captured images of the couple formerly known as "the Poison Penns." This time, Madonna and Sean seemed unconcerned, immersed in each other's company.

15. I'm Breathless

Madonna had already finished her next album when she began working with Alek Keshishian on her "Blonde Ambition" documentary.

Without a doubt, Warren Beatty knew that getting Madonna as an actress would be an added advantage to Dick Tracy: the chance of her participating in the soundtrack of his film. A film studio would consider the release of a Madonna single several weeks before the release of a film in which she is involved to be millions of dollars in promotion. When Warren Beatty cast Madonna as the gold-digging Breathless Mahoney, Disney (the film's distributor) gained the benefit of having a hugely popular pop star on the soundtrack, and Warner Bros. Records had a reason to release Madonna's seventh album, I'm Breathless (Music from and Inspired by the Film Dick Tracy), in May 1990.

Madonna's CD would include three songs from the film that she recorded. Her actual challenge, however, would be to develop and produce new songs for the collection, songs with an authentic lyrical/musical relationship to the film. As a result, the album's subtitle, Music from and Inspired by the Film Dick Tracy, was chosen. The three songs Madonna would record were penned by theatre master Stephen Sondheim, thus it would be a challenging task. As a result, the new songs Madonna chooses to record must be at least stylistically close to his. In Madonna's favour, she would have a hand in producing the entire album, including the Sondheim songs, and her involvement would assure some degree of consistency. Madonna enlisted the assistance of Patrick Leonard (her most dependable studio ally) and recording engineer-turned-producer Bill Bottrell (whose work with Madonna would serve him well in securing production jobs with Michael Jackson and pop rocker Sheryl Crow).

Madonna and Leonard worked hard to create music that fit the mood and attitude of the picture, which is set during prohibition in the days of The Untouchables. As Warren Beatty described it, they were successful "beyond my wildest dreams." Madonna and Leonard kick off the album with "He's a Man," a big, dramatic, vamping bluesy ballad that Madonna sings as if she's a hooker stalking the boulevard. She has an amazing voice. "I want people to think of me as a musical comedy actress," she remarked back then. "For me, that's what this record is about. It's a bit of a stretch. Not simply pop music, but songs with a particular vibe, a theatrical vibe." Indeed, she addressed the Sondheim songs with the zeal of a Broadway veteran, including the dark, resolute "Sooner or Later," the modified ragtime of "More," and the gentle, tender wonder, "What Can You Lose?" Madonna holds her own, especially during "What Can You Lose," a duet with Mandy Patinkin, her voice first appearing on the tune like a flower blossoming at dawn, warming to the mission at hand. One can question what a singer like Barbra Streisand would have brought to the production that Madonna did not, but such contemplation does not detract from Madonna's performance, which is genuinely wonderful.

In comparison, Andy Paley's "I'm Going Bananas" is like delicious taffy, a Ricky Ricardo type of song that Madonna delivers completely in Breathless character. Then, as if to say, "Hey, I can do that, too," she and Leonard created "Cry Baby," a witty Roaring Twenties ballad that Madonna performs as Betty Boop. When Madonna and Leonard get up to make "Something to Remember," both tunes, which were pure fun and games, sound like filler. The ballad is complex and sad, sailing on a tide of lovely, mournful chords and wandering melodies that quietly make it the most fascinating thing Madonna has ever dedicated her voice to. If anyone ever questions the lady's musical integrity, she can simply point to the composition for "Something to Remember" – that would be enough to silence even the most accomplished composer.

Madonna also managed to provide substance to what appeared to be the lightest of moments. The steamrolling "Hanky Panky" appears to be a lighthearted harmless romp until you understand what she's talking about is "Warren's favourite pastime"... being paddled! It's tough to listen to I'm Breathless and not feel forced to search for the true Madonna in each song. She is, without a question, more brilliant than Breathless Mahoney, but both possessed the drive and determination required to achieve their goals. Consider this: Madonna was a rising dance-music artist with big dreams. In less than ten years, she was a prominent movie co-star, singing a lighthearted duet — "Now I'm Following You" — with Warren Beatty on the soundtrack record!

Even though I'm Breathless was a success, it lacked a musical hook: a hit song. To that purpose, Madonna and Shep Pettibone (the great engineer/songwriter/producer who has always stood in the shadow of Madonna's constant collaborators Steve Bray and Patrick Leonard) concocted "Vogue," a sleek tune that Madonna would co-write and produce. It's a funky, uptown anthem glorifying the art of "voguing" — a popular dance at the time that was more about posing like a high-fashion model than working out. Actually, voguing has been there long before Madonna sang about it; like Michael Jackson and his "Moonwalk," dance, Madonna simply promoted it to the rest of the world. The unforgettable throbbing music was a brilliant dance tribute to "Ladies with attitude, fellows who were in the mood" (with an accompanying iconic black-and-white film that was undoubtedly influenced by famous images taken by Horst of Hollywood stars). The "Vogue rap" remains one of Madonna's most memorable camp musical moments ("Greta Garbo and Monroe, Dietrich and DiMaggio...").

According to Madonna historian Bruce Baron, "Vogue" was originally intended as the B side of the "Keep It Together" record. When Warner execs heard the song, they opted to release it as an A side. According to Baron, Madonna had to change some of the more provocative lyrics because the song was to be placed on an album associated with a Disney film.

"Vogue" achieved what Madonna and Shep Pettibone had hoped for: it reached number one. (Her spectacular performance of the song on the MTV Video Music Awards in 1990, dressed as Marie Antoinette in a giant hoop-skirt suit with loads of cleavage, a bouffant hairstyle, and white-powder makeup, was a legendary camp spectacle that raised the bar for subsequent performances on that show.)

Then, following "Vogue," "Hanky Panky" made a respectable ascent to Number. Both singles helped propel I'm Breathless to the number two spot on Billboard's album chart. It sold two million copies in the United States and five million worldwide.

I'm Breathless is one of Madonna's best musical moments, a quite bold statement given her prodigious recording history. "I worked so hard on that record," she explained afterward. "In its time and place, it's important to me." Also, Warren Beatty couldn't have been happier, and as her friends recall, she wanted nothing more than his approval for all of her work in film, acting, and singing. "He meant a lot to her," Freddy DeMann confirms. "She wanted him to be proud."

Warren's thoughts toward the record may have been revealed when he co-hosted a party at his home with Madonna shortly after its release. He instructed her to "dress down" for his Hollywood pals Jack Nicholson, Michelle Pfeiffer, and Al Pacino, as well as the studio heads of various film firms, the so-called movers and shakers of the industry.

Madonna frequently remarked on Warren's "people skills." It was true in 1990, and it is still true today, that his warm, firm handclasp as he turns his attention to someone often leaves that person with the impression that he or she has been touched by something unique.

Madonna noted how people were energised by any meeting with Warren, genuinely delighted to be in his company. It was a different scenario with her: unless they were true fans, most people were afraid of her when they met her, scared about what she would say or do to them. People crowded around her when she went into a room, not because they wanted to touch her, but because they wanted to see what crazy event would occur as a result of her presence, who she would insult, and what swear word she would speak while doing it. She stated that she wanted to learn how to be more courteous from Warren. As a result, gatherings at Warren's were always exciting for Madonna; she relished the company of his powerful show-biz buddies and appreciated how they treated her, accepting her as one of their own.

Madonna donned a simple, bare-back black Halston gown to the Dick Tracy celebration, with her golden hair in a subtle twist. She had a feminine, fitted, graceful, and sophisticated appearance. She appeared to be an experienced socialite, as she smiled, touched, kissed, and moved through the crowd. She was casually conversing with folks who normally bored her. Warren's jokes made her laugh out loud. She didn't curse. Did she ever imagine she'd be so near to the magic, power, and glamour of true Hollywood, and how well she'd fit in? Most likely, yeah. "She was delightful," a guest remarked, "the perfect hostess."

Warren played "Something to Remember," from the Dick Tracy soundtrack, during the party and requested his guests to stop talking long enough to listen to the music. Everyone complied. Certainly, Madonna must have felt a little embarrassed during these few minutes as she stood with a martini in one hand, a cigarette in the other... with all eyes on her. Even the battalion of tuxedo-clad waiters, stationed like toy soldiers with trays of crudités, pâtés, and other appetisers, took attention.

When the song ended, Warren approached Madonna and said

something to her. She answered with a surprised smile and what appeared to be an appreciative nod. Then, with a flourish, he turned away from her and started applauding. His guests followed his lead, showering Madonna with cheers, smiles, and words of congratulations. It had to have been a once-in-a-lifetime experience for her. "She stood there and just accepted it all graciously... this beautiful, unpredictable, amazing young woman with tears in her eyes," Jack Nicholson later said. What a shining star."

16. Warren Proposes Marriage to Madonna?

It was 1990. Madonna would turn 32 in a few months. Her career had been fantastic in many respects up until this point. Her personal life, however, has been less than pleasant, particularly her love interactions with males. Each had been motivated, for the most part, by immense and overwhelming emotion — either intense lovemaking or fierce bickering. There was no room for compromise. Madonna, like her father and then Sean Penn, seemed to believe that a relationship was not legitimate unless it entailed yelling and shouting. She couldn't stop starting arguments with her lovers even in public. She appeared unable to comprehend the concept of loving a man yet disagreeing with him without participating in an endless and loud argument about it.

No one Madonna had ever been romantically engaged with did much to support her emotional needs in the past. Of course, many people had helped her on her way to prominence. She eventually flung those men aside after she was done with them. Those who had attempted to assist her in dealing with her emotional issues were also pushed away. Despite being incapable of actual closeness, she managed to attract men like Sean Penn, John Kennedy, and now Warren Beatty, all of whom were as inept.

Her love life was about to get even more complicated...

Warren Beatty made a stunning move on May 16, over a romantic meal at a Hollywood restaurant after a long day of dubbing in the studio. He either asked Madonna for her hand in marriage (as she told her friends) or he asked her to consent to marry him one day (as he clumsily characterised the offer to his friends). Whatever his proposal, he gave her a six-carat, $30,000 diamond and sapphire ring.

Madonna slid the ring on the middle finger of her left hand, apparently to conceal the fact that it represented a promise of marriage, while wearing a long straight blonde wig parted in the middle and what appeared to be a man's classic pinstripe suit with a bustier. The pair hailed the occasion after Warren signalled the server to replenish their glasses of Cristal champagne. Warren was so overjoyed that Madonna had accepted his ring that he tipped the server — one of the sources for this story — $500.

Most of their acquaintances had to agree that Madonna and Warren's vow — whether it was a genuine engagement or an agreement to one day become engaged — didn't seem to bring them any closer as a pair; they continued to argue.

"Keep your stupid opinions to yourself," Madonna told Warren at dinner at the Ivy in Los Angeles a few days after the "engagement." The reason for the fight is unknown. Beatty threw a handful of cash onto the table, appearing irritated. He stood up. He walked away. A disgruntled Madonna was left alone to stew, with roughly fifty amused patrons staring at her. "Stop staring at me," she yelled before storming out.

Warren and Madonna stayed at the opulent La Mansion del Rio Hotel in San Antonio, Texas, for a weekend studio promotional obligation. Warren de-stressed by golfing in between press appearances, while Madonna indulged in daily facials and other forms of pampering. "Warren spent the weekend on the phone to Jack [Nicholson] complaining about Madonna, that she and Sandra Bernhard were planning a big wedding, that Sean Penn was calling him every fifteen minutes screaming at him to leave his ex-wife alone," said Bill Hollerman, Beatty's golfing buddy. It just kept going. Beatty stated that she was not content unless she was arguing with him. 'She's a nice girl, but you can't take her out,' he said. You never know what she'll say or do next. You have no idea what the next major fight will be about. 'I'm getting too old for this.'"

"But you're not that old," his pal pointed out.

"Well, I'm old enough to not want to look foolish," she replied.

According to Hollerman, one of Beatty's ex-girlfriends, Barbra Streisand, was also on the phone to Texas, telling him that he was "crazy for falling for a young floozy." "When she heard about Warren and Madonna, she became a great instigator," says a former business associate of Barbra's. Prior to that announcement, she and Warren had little to do with each other, but now she became his great protector, informing him that Madonna was merely using him to boost her film career.In addition, his elderly mother, Kathleen, who was still a significant influence in his life, did not approve of Madonna. "No matter how hard Madonna tried, she was unable to impress the older woman."

An unexpected breaking point occurred when Madonna gave Warren a costly oil painting as a gift. He politely thanked her and stowed it under the couch, where he most likely meant for it to stay because it didn't match his decor. After three days, Madonna decided to hang the picture on the wall in his living room. Warren exploded at her when he saw it displayed without his authorization, accusing her of attempting to "control" him. The combat continued from there. It was a minor occurrence, but it ignited something in Warren and Madonna, resulting in a fight large enough to derail whatever future plans they had.

***

Dick Tracy aired in June 1990, and after all the excitement, it appeared to be the success Disney had predicted. It debuted to strong box office receipts. (In the end, however, the film was a financial flop, grossing only $104 million in the United States.)

Madonna was dissatisfied with how her production numbers were chopped; she has stated that she refused to see the entire film because she couldn't face seeing how her routines were cut (she has yet to see it). Warren believed she was being foolish, which fueled their argument even more. Things were especially strained between the pair when Warren refused to appear on the cover of Newsweek magazine unless he was shown alone. When Newsweek's editor-in-chief Rick Smith notified Disney studio director Jeffery Katzenberg that there would be no cover profile without Madonna, he quickly ordered that a photograph of Madonna be supplied to the magazine. Still, Madonna thought Warren was being disloyal by attempting to cut her out of a major magazine cover, and the two got into another disagreement, this time about publicity.

"I was in Florida with Warren [for further Dick Tracy promotion] when a call came in from Madonna," one business acquaintance and friend of Beatty's says. 'I'm working,' he explained. We were playing golf. That told me the story."

"Do you love her?" Warren's friend inquired while the two were playing golf.

Warren seems perplexed by the question. "She's a lot of fun," he remarked. "But what exactly is love?" I truly don't think I understand. "My problem," he said, "is that I get bored easily."

"I wasn't encouraged by his response," his associate now admits. I understood right away that they were not going to marry, but he did say he had asked Jack Nicholson to be his best man if he ever married her. He also stated that she had requested Sandra Bernhard to serve as her maid of honour. That seems like a really good show, but maybe not such a wonderful marriage, I thought. By his demeanour, I knew it would never happen."

According to some onlookers, Warren had been worn down by Madonna's arrogance. Perhaps the fact that he gave her a symbolic ring said more about his inner turmoil than it did about his affections for Madonna. He was like an impulsive, reckless high schooler attempting to impress his sweetheart with a costly, ostentatious gift. When it came time to live up to the promise symbolised by that ring, Warren was unable to meet the challenge – he couldn't commit, just as he hadn't committed to so many other women in the past. If anyone was going to influence Warren Beatty's life path, it wasn't Madonna. Her actions simply made him flee in the opposite direction.

"Where have you been?" According to Bill Hollerman, Madonna demanded to know about Warren. After a day of golfing, the two had just walked into her suite. Madonna sipped tea at her workstation, which faced a wall. She was dressed in a white cottony terry cloth robe. Her hair was wrapped in a matching towel. She wore no makeup and appeared to have just showered. "She looked about twelve," Hollerman recalled. "Thirteen, tops."

"Oh, we were golfing," Warren explained. Given her demanding tone, he appeared perplexed that he should have to react.

"But we were supposed to have lunch," she pointed out, rising to face him. She was having a bad day.

"Well, that's what I'm here for now, to have lunch."

Madonna removed the towel off her hair and began drying it. "And who is this?" she wondered. She nodded towards Bill Hollerman without ever looking him in the eyes.

"He'll be joining us. "Do you mind if I ask?"

She produced a glum expression. "Yes, I mind," she stated unequivocally. "I never eat with strangers." Warren, you are aware of this." Madonna walked into the restroom and closed the door behind her. After a brief pause, she exclaimed from the other room, "For all I know, he works for the fucking National Enquirer, and you want me to fucking eat with him?"

"Charming, isn't she?" Warren told Bill. The two gentlemen exited her suite.

According to Beatty's pal, Madonna called Warren on his cell phone when he was on the golf course the next day. Beatty cringed as he held the phone approximately two feet from his ear. Her speech was like chalk on a blackboard, scratching on his nerves.

Despite the fact that the relationship was clearly doomed, Madonna looked anxious to keep Warren Beatty. People in her group knew her to have an addicted disposition when it comes to males at the time. She appeared to become "hooked" on the drama of whichever relationship she was in at the time. The fact that she and Warren had such nasty disagreements appears to be what brought them together. It was the same type of drama that had kept her connected to Sean Penn long after their relationship should have ended. While it may not have been a wonderful relationship, it was still a connection... her method of holding on to Sean. Madonna now desired to preserve whatever she had with Warren.

While discussing some of her "issues," her friend, millionaire entrepreneur David Geffen, suggested she see a psychiatrist, and after a few meetings, Madonna appeared to be on the verge of exploding with psychoanalysis in an interview with Vanity Fair. "I admit that I have this feeling that I'm a bad girl and I need to be punished," she went on to say. "There's a part of me that says, 'Fuck you!'" You're a jerk! I'm throwing this in your face!' is the part that's covering up the part that's saying, 'I'm hurt. And now that I've been abandoned, I'll never need anyone again.' "I've also not resolved my Electra complex," she continued, unprompted.

"The end of the 'Oh Father' video, where I'm dancing on my mother's grave, is an attempt to embrace and accept my mother's death." "I had to deal with the loss of my mother, and then I had to deal with the guilt of her absence, and then I had to deal with the loss of my father when he married my stepmother," she noted. So I was simply a lonely, furious girl. "I'm still enraged."

17. Sex

Time-Warner published Madonna's infamous book, Sex, on October 21, 1992. After months of anticipation and expectation, the public found that Madonna's first excursion into publishing would be a large and costly ($49.95), 128-page volume spiral-bound between embossed stainless-steel covers, suitably titled, simply, Sex. To guarantee that the public understood the contentious nature of this publishing venture, the book arrived in bookstores wrapped in silver Mylar (which also ensured that only paying customers could see what was between its covers). A CD of Madonna's new single, "Erotica," was also included in a silver Mylar Ziplock bag. "Warner Books is shitting in their pants about it," Freddy DeMann remarked of the publishing house's apprehension about disseminating such a novel.

Some may argue that the origins of Madonna's Sex reveal a typical aspect of her personality and the way she, as she has stated in the past, "takes a little of this and that and turns it into my own." Judith Regan, then an editor at Simon & Schuster Pocket Books, had an idea for a book of erotica and sexual fantasies that she thought Madonna would like in the fall of 1990. "I felt that it was right in line with what she was all about at that time," Regan said. "So I sent a box of material to her manager's office, which included erotic photos I thought she'd like as well as text I thought would be appropriate." If I do say so myself, it was colourful and imaginative. In any case, I was satisfied. As it turned out, she was impressed as well and thought it was a terrific idea. I was in Los Angeles the next thing I know, sitting with her and her manager, Freddy DeMann. I was pregnant at the time, and Madonna's first words to me were, 'Well, you know, I don't have any children.' It seemed strange that she would think I wouldn't know anything about one of the world's most famous women."

"I just want you to know that if you've offered it to even one other celebrity, I won't even think of doing it," Madonna warned Judith Regan during their meeting.

"Why is that?" Judith inquired. Of course, she knew the answer, but she wanted to hear it directly from the woman.

"Because it has to be unique to me," Madonna explained. "It has to be for me, and for me alone."

"I started at the top." "I'll be with you," Judith told her. "If you're not interested, I'll go somewhere else." But I hope you'll be intrigued. I believe this could be very beneficial to you."

Madonna appeared content. Throughout the conversation, she made it clear that she would only take on such a project if she had complete control over it. "She has amazing instincts, I learned that right away about her," Regan said. "She knew exactly what she wanted to do and how to go about it." She asked insightful publishing questions. Not surprisingly, I found her to be quite enthusiastic and highly intelligent. Shrewd."

Perhaps Madonna was more cunning than Judith thought. By the end of the discussion, she had agreed "in principle" to write a book titled Madonna's Book of Erotica and Sexual Fantasies, according to Judith. She stated that her manager will contact me and we would finalise the details. I never heard from her again and concluded that she simply did not want to do it. Six months later, I discovered she was working on the project for Warner Books [a division of Time-Warner that owns Warner Bros. Records and currently distributes Madonna's record label, Maverick]. She had definitely copied my concept, images, and ideas and utilised them as a pitch to another publisher. "I never heard from her, not a word of gratitude, apology, or anything," Judith Regan concludes. "Frankly, I thought it was in poor taste."

When it was finally published, the contents of Sex consisted of visual and verbal essays by Madonna (as herself, but also in the role of a character named Dita, based on the 1930s screen goddess Dita Parlo) about her personal, sexual fantasies — or, at least, what she wanted the public to believe were her sexual fantasies. "This book does not condone unsafe sex," she quickly added in one of her letters to the reader. "These are fantasies I made up." When I let my mind wander, like most people, I rarely think of condoms."

Madonna was seen hitchhiking in the nude, posing lasciviously while clad in leather S&M outfits, brutally dominating a pair of butch lesbians, happily sucking someone's toe, brazenly shaving someone else's pubic area, receiving oral sex from a biker, and being viciously raped by skin-heads (while dressed as a schoolgirl). In most of the images, she is at least partially naked, and in many of them, she is entirely naked. In one of them, she is seen in a sexually suggestive attitude with a dog. "It turned out to be a lot more salacious, I think, than what I would have wanted to publish," Regan explains. "She went overboard with it. I wanted it to be inventive, sexy... yet not too obscene."

Much of the book, in fact, reads like a letter to a pornographic magazine: "I love my pussy, it is the complete summation of my life," she added. "My pussy is the temple of learning." A lot of emphasis is also placed on the pleasure of anal intercourse, which is described as "the most pleasurable way to [have sex], and it also hurts the most." Many graphic paragraphs are devoted to the various ways she enjoys making love, with each position described in exquisite detail, much of it involving sadomasochism. She also waxes poetic about her first masturbation.

Much of Sex is unexpected, if not shocking. Instead of being an "adult" book, it is infantile and impetuous. Though Madonna insisted that she was attempting to demystify sexuality in all of its guises, knowing who she was and how she operated revealed to any keen observer that what she was really trying to get away with was as much naughty-girl text and as many pornographic photographs as she could get away with because... well, because she could get away with it. She was behaving like a brat, not like a revolutionary. That much is evident if one reads between the lines of a 1998 MTV interview she conducted. "I thought, 'You know what, I'm going to be sexually provocative, I'm going to be ironic, and I'm going to prove that I can get everybody's attention and that everyone's going to be interested in it . . . and still be freaked out about it.'" Why, one could ask? Hadn't she previously proven her sexually provocative, ironic, and attention-grabbing abilities?

Those who knew Madonna well understood what was actually going on with her at the time: the Sex book — and the outlandish antics that before and will follow it — was only a barrier between her and the rest of the world.

For years, Madonna felt as if every minute of her life had been exposed to the world, with her every word and emotion splashed across the media for remark, often harsh and negative. She felt hunted, despite the fact that she had initiated the pursuit. She had made herself one of the most watched and criticised women in the world. She had never disappointed her audience, always ready with a provocative remark, a scandalous narrative, or a startling snapshot. She was having problems relating to "normal" people now because she was just who she had created. She had the impression that they didn't comprehend her. And she had no idea what they meant. She seems to have become lost among all the headlines. Her ironic fate was terrible loneliness, the result of being such a fantastic public character. Her interactions with guys had been horrible. Was some of that due to her celebrity?

To avoid having to be a part of the crowd, either consciously or subconsciously — only she knows which — Madonna crafted a persona that no one could comprehend. ... one so ridiculous as to defy understanding, one that most people (at least those who were not pornographers) found repulsive. "She was losing touch," one of her publicists explained. "The barrier she put up between herself and the rest of the world was the notion of crazy, wild sex — pure and simple — and trashy and controversial sex."

Most mental health practitioners believe that there are two ways to be antisocial in the human condition. It might manifest as aggressive, antagonistic conduct in men. It can be presented as sexually provocative and outlandish in a lady. In other words, when little boys are irritated, they fight. When tiny girls get furious, they expose their underwear. Some of us never grow out of it; it appears like Madonna was "showing her panties" simply because she was irritated by the enormous scrutiny her personal life had received over the years. She saw no other option except to fight back.

Tony Ward, Naomi Campbell, Isabella Rosellini, and rappers Big Daddy Kane and Vanilla Ice all appeared in the Sex book in images in various degrees of nakedness.

The photos were taken throughout the course of an eight-month romance between Madonna and Vanilla Ice (actual name Rob Van Winkle). Ice, whose song "Ice Ice Baby" became the first rap song to top the Billboard charts in 1990, admits that his connection with Madonna was challenging "because she would change personalities a lot." He also says he now regrets posing with her for the book. "It kind of cheeses me out," he confesses. "It makes me look like everyone else in there, a bunch of freaks." "I'm not a freak."

Madonna's friend Ingrid Casares was also prominently featured, however she later complained that her participation in the project would fuel years of fanciful talk about her own sex life. "I'm actually quite conservative," Casares declares unequivocally. Casares and Madonna were spotted kissing passionately in male drag.

Though the book's initial popularity sent it to the top of The New York Times best-seller list, the reviews were mainly unfavourable. The Washington Post's Richard Harrington described it as "an oversized, overpriced coffee-table book of hard-core sexual fantasies certain to separate the wanna-bes from the wanna-be-far-away." Is Sex upsetting? Not at all. Mostly because it's Madonna, and we've learned to expect nothing less from her. Is sex monotonous? In fact, sure."

With all the sexual posturing, it was ironic that Madonna was seen in Penny Marshall's light comedic frolic, A club of Their Own, about a women's baseball club in 1943, in the summer of 1992. Madonna would not have to shoulder the weight of an entire picture as part of an all-star group that included Geena Davis, Tom Hanks, and Rosie O'Donnell. The film was the highest-grossing film of the summer of 1992, adding to Madonna's acting resume – albeit she was only fair in the role, and most people don't remember it. Any observer who hoped the film would herald the birth of a tamed Madonna realised he was mistaken as soon as Sex was released.

18. Erotica

Madonna launched a new album, Erotica, to coincide with the release of Sex.

It's a shame that Erotica had to be associated with less memorable undertakings in Madonna's career at this time, because, unlike Truth or Dare and Sex, Erotica had a lot to recommend it. It was merely that, coming on the heels of the previous two projects, Erotica appeared to most onlookers to be more of the same. However, because it has actual value, this album should be assessed on its own merits, not just as one tied to the other two adult-oriented initiatives.

Madonna has frequently stated that, in her opinion, and that of many cultural historians, one of the reasons pop music is so strong in society is because it frequently serves as a mirror of our civilization. Perusing the Billboard Top 40 could be an excellent place to start if one wants to know what's going on in the world. While newspapers provide daily information, pop music, at least on certain levels, can provide a larger picture. For example, there may be no songs in the Top 40 advocating peace, love, or improving society; if so, their absence speaks loudly. It could imply that society is turning a blind eye at the moment, preferring to trade its difficulties for a nice pop ballad about happy times and romance. Apathy and hopefulness, optimism and good cheer – wherever mainstream culture is at the time, music is usually there as well.

Few singers have their fingers on the pulse of society like Madonna, more so than Michael Jackson (who looks to spend too much time in his own environment to be in touch) or Prince (who appears to be too self-obsessed to pay attention to anything else). Madonna's instincts keep her connected to life.

When Erotica was released in October 1992, much of society appeared to be rethinking its sexuality. Gay rights issues were at the centre of global social conversations, as was a growing awareness of AIDS. A generation seems increasingly interested in exploring, without guilt, shame, or apology, a different slice of life, something more provocative, perhaps darker... including Erotica themes. A concept album in certain ways, its music was more freely and proudly centred on sexuality than any previous Madonna album. Erotica was more than just boy meets girl and birds and bees. Madonna has already skillfully expressed similar naive sentiments in pop songs like the effervescent "Cherish" and the sincere "Open Your Heart." Erotica was darker, franker, and more edgy. Madonna must have known that the timing was ideal for an album of her calibre. (She also believed, evidently, that it was time for a book that would address these topics — thus her Sex book. While hearing Madonna's perspective on sexuality is a positive experience, seeing it page after page after page is not.

Anyone who had been paying attention to Madonna's recent music may have predicted Erotica. She had already shown her hand with Breathless when she sang "Hanky Panky," the spanking song, with a little too much power. Then there was her track "Justify My Love," a very sinister piece of sexiness. Erotica, on the other hand, was a full-fledged musical inquiry, an exposition of Madonna's sexual reality.

Madonna returned to producer/writer Shep Pettibone for this album, with whom she had previously written and produced "Vogue." Madonna wanted to do a clear and obvious dance song after having to work within the musical confines of Breathless; Pettibone was skilled in this genre. Indeed, based on the music they've made together, it's safe to say Pettibone is by far her best dance-music partner. Madonna would sculpt the vocal melody and create the lyrics after he laid down the musical tracks. She's so versatile that she often has suggestions for music tracks (like on Erotica). They get along great because he understands her. "She's the polar opposite of calm," Pettibone says. "Because her patience is extremely low, you must ensure that everything runs smoothly." Because the beast isn't much fun, it's preferable to bring out the angel in her."

It wasn't necessary to listen to the music to comprehend Madonna's goal with Erotica. If the title wasn't a dead giveaway, the artwork on the CD's cover certainly was. One photograph from Sex shows Madonna in S&M costume, toying with a riding crop and sucking her arm; another shows her bound and gagged. The back cover depicts Madonna engaging in "foot worship" - contentedly sucking on someone's big toe. However, her public would have been startled by the stances in her Sex book; however, on the heels of that published work, these images suddenly felt redundant.

The title track, which was also the album's first single, had an addictive house-music beat over which Madonna, in her "Mistress Dita" persona, spoke in a mesmerising, orgasmic way about the relationship between pain and pleasure and how it relates to sex. The spoken lines are broken up by the hypnotic, seductive chorus, "Erotic, erotic, put your hands all over my body." The song might have easily been the theme song for a Fellini film.

MTV swiftly put the "Erotica" video on "heavy rotation"... after midnight, of course, to safeguard the kids. Madonna appears on TV as a disguised dominatrix, complete with gold teeth and slicked-back hair. She tongue-kisses a female and performs her S&M routine, but it is cut too abruptly to be truly revealing. The film seemed to be more about generating a shocking picture montage. The normally clean-cut man looked out of place in leather and sunglasses. "Some people have no objection to such role-playing games as long as they're consensual," MTV announcer Kurt Loder teased. Others find such actions repugnant, which is why MTV is not showing this video during regular daytime or evening programming."

Molly Ivins, the author of the column, wrote, "You could tell you're out of touch with your fellow Americans when the reigning sex goddess is someone you wouldn't take home if she were the last woman left in the bar."

This time, a more subdued Madonna did not appear to be bothered by MTV's reduction of screen time for her video. "MTV has a huge audience, and a lot of them are kids," she stated in an interview with the cable network. "And a lot of the themes explored in my video aren't meant for children, so I understand why they can't show it."

Of course, Madonna's fans were even more captivated by the song and video as a result of the controversy. It peaked at No. 1 on the Billboard singles list.

"Deeper and Deeper," Erotica's second single, was a departure from the title track. The single featured Madonna speaking conventional lyrics about falling hard for a lover over a straight-ahead house rhythm in the manner of the funkiest New York clubs. It climbed to number seven on the chart.

Erotica was possibly ahead of its time. Madonna's song "Secret Garden," with its lyrics spoken over a jazz combo, is reminiscent of the cool soul music that groups like the Roots and Erykah Badu would popularise almost a decade later under the title of "neo-soul." Erotica was a musical melting pot of nineties urban music, combining developing hip hop and house with a more traditional synthesiser-based rhythm and blues. Madonna's most sexually provocative album was also her most R&B-influenced.

However, it was the spectacle of the artist's sensuality on display that had both admirers and critics gasping for air. Erotica was the first (and so far only) Madonna CD to bear the disclaimer "Parental Advisory: Explicit Lyrics." Obviously, Madonna did not develop the images of S&M and bondage that she so heroically exploited, but one could argue that Erotica was a soundtrack for the era's sexual liberation as individuals tried to still enjoy their sexuality despite the fear of AIDS. Unlike her novel, this music was an art form that her audience would not be weary of... and to which they might return for entertainment. However, in keeping with Madonna's self-inflicted career slump at the time, Erotica was the least commercially successful of her releases, selling just over two million copies.

"Most people want to hear me say I'm sorry I published my Sex book." "I don't," Madonna said to Time magazine a few years later. "What was difficult was releasing my Erotica album at the same time." That was an underappreciated record in my opinion. My book eclipsed everything I did for the next three years."

19. Bad Career Moves

By the end of 1992, many of Madonna's followers and critics were wondering if she had gone too far. For some, the publication of the Truth or Dare film, the Sex book, and the Erotica music and video answered that question with a loud "Yes!" (In the United States, Truth or Dare grossed only $15 million. Madonna invested $4 million in the film as executive producer, therefore she did make a profit. After expenses, however, the picture was not nearly as profitable as she had intended.)

Who, after all, was this woman? Was she a sexual outcast, or just a pampered, internationally renowned brat who liked to strip naked and talk dirty? No one could give an accurate answer since she had covered her genuine identity with scandal and sensationalism. Even when she tried to justify herself ("I love my pussy, and there's nothing wrong with loving my pussy"), she came out as a lustful porn actress no one could take seriously.

"After the Sex book came out," she said in her memoir, "there was a time when I could not open up a newspaper or magazine and not read something incredibly scathing about myself."

If Madonna had known the terrible press that Truth or Dare, Sex and Erotica would generate, she would have chosen a different approach for her next picture, possibly continuing with light family-oriented films like A League of Their Own. Instead, she chose a gruesome thriller, Body of Evidence, as her next film release – the final of four unintentional steps in the demise of her career.

Madonna stars as Rebecca Carlson, a gallery owner accused of murdering a wealthy older man after he dies after having sex with her (raising the perplexing question of whether or not a sex partner's body can be considered a lethal weapon if the act results in a person's death). She eventually becomes physically connected with her defence attorney, Willem Dafoe.

Madonna's character is slain at the end of the film, which some outraged audiences applaud. "She's a powerful lady," says Uli Edel, the film's director, of Madonna. "Sometimes you feel like a tamer with a caged she-lion." You must force her to leap through this burning hoop, and there are only two options. She'll either jump into the ring of fire... or she'll murder you."

"In every movie from the 1940s, the bad girl has to die," Madonna has declared. "What I liked about the role [in the original script] was that she didn't die." They eventually killed me. As a result, I felt sabotaged to some level. For some reason, when that movie came out, I was held fully accountable for it. It was entirely my fault, which was preposterous given that we all make awful movies. I mean, Diabolique was released [in 1996], and Sharon Stone was not held accountable for the fact that it was a bad film."

Indeed, critics "murdered" Madonna in their reviews, calling Body of Evidence a third-rate retread of every murder mystery of the previous twenty years (especially Basic Instinct, the year before's box-office smash). Reviewers were quick to draw comparisons between Madonna and the film's main lady: "It's not just that Madonna does not make an effective Sharon Stone," a Rolling Stone critic grumbled. "She's not even a convincing Madonna." Madonna takes positions and delivers awkward sentences that seem like captions from her book Sex read aloud in a nerve-jangling stridency."

Bad press and condemnation of religious groups had never hurt Madonna's career before this point, but when it was revealed that moviegoers were laughing out loud at Madonna's ostensibly serious characterization in Body of Evidence, it became clear that she had pushed the envelope as far as it could go. Even though she realised that if she was going to be able to establish a career, she needed to reinvent herself, especially after another picture, Dangerous Game, was released (in 1993) to poor reviews and a dismal box office. Madonna is an actress with little talents who has sex with almost everyone in her life in this one. The intercourse is brutal - Madonna gets to strip multiple times and does so enthusiastically. During one scene in Dangerous Game, James Russo remarks of Madonna's character, Sarah Jennings, "We both know she's a fucking whore who can't act." Again, it was all too much for reviewers — or her audience. What a letdown, especially given that it was directed by the highly regarded Abel Ferrara (known at the time for The Bad Lieutenant, starring Harvey Keitel, who also co-starred in Dangerous Game) and that Madonna had funded a large portion of it herself.

Meanwhile, fortunately for her, Madonna's recording and performing career had maintained enough momentum to overcome the dip caused by such ventures as Body of Evidence and Dangerous Game. Madonna chose not to hide from the onslaught of publicity. Instead, she did what she'd always done best: she put her show on the road.

Madonna embarked on a restricted twenty-date, four-continent globe tour in the fourth quarter of 1993, dubbed "The Girlie Show." She wisely knew that a total career turnaround would be obvious, and would likely devalue much of what she had done prior to this point. She had successfully raised the awareness of a large portion of her audience, even if her methods were occasionally questionable. If she was going to create a new image, the shift would have to be gradual. As a result, "The Girlie Show" was a stopover tour. While still attractive, it was more of a harmless burlesque than a brazen attempt to shock. The previous two years' hard core S&M imagery and heretical religious iconography were gone. This concert, on the other hand, had the air of a raucous Barnum and Bailey circus, even displaying a softer, gentler Madonna.

Times described it as, "At once a movie retrospective, a Ziegfeld revue, a living video, an R-rated takeoff on Cirque du Soleil — opens with Smokey Robinson's 'Tears of a Clown' and closes with

Cole Porter's 'Be a Clown.'" According to the magazine, Madonna, "once the Harlow harlot and now a perky harlequin, is the greatest show-off on earth." "The Girlie Show" allowed Madonna to cap off a challenging year on a high note. Many commentators and fans thought it was her best presentation to date, reaffirming that Madonna could still impress her audience as a singer and stage performer, if not as a movie star. Still, she was more sensitive to criticism than ever before, possibly because she'd had to deal with so much of it recently. Even a tiny unfavourable tone in a review would throw her into a tailspin. "No one understands me," she lamented to a close friend. "I'm not following the rules. "How come people don't get it?"

"Maybe because people are sick to death of you and all of the sex nonsense," stated one of the friends. "Even toned down, it's still too much." Madonna did not speak to that person for the next six months.

20. Trash Talking on TV

During the "The Girlie Show" tour, Madonna had a heated phone discussion with her father, Tony, during which he begged her to "stop being so racy." According to what Madonna later revealed to close friends, he was embarrassed not by what she was doing, but by what people were saying about her. Rather than empathising with what her father was presumably trying to communicate, which was that outsiders criticising his daughter damaged his feelings, she misinterpreted his comment. The two were suddenly immersed in the same conflict they had been battling for years, over Madonna's perception that her father had never supported or understood her art. Or, as Tony later put it, "When a father is involved, does that mean he doesn't approve?" Why is she such a jerk? "What gives her the right to take everything so personally?"

Even after all these years, Madonna was still so wounded and angry by her mother's death that there was nothing Tony Ciccone could say or do that would be acceptable to her. It was the usual story: she needed someone to blame for her loss, so she blamed her father. Nonetheless, she wants his praise.

Tony had to have been worried when he saw his daughter on The Late Show with David Letterman on March 31, 1994.

Madonna's recent realisation that startling the public to build interest in herself was no longer working must have been bolstered when she observed the audience's reaction to her on the Letterman show. She appeared on Holy Thursday night, when Catholics commemorate the Last Supper during the Easter season.

Madonna humiliated herself on Letterman's show nearly from the moment she sat down, possibly in a last-ditch attempt to be provocative, sexy, and controversial. She stepped onto the platform holding a pair of panties while dressed in a tight black velvet dress with matching scarred combat boots. Within seconds, she had started into what many saw as an offensive performance, complete with a torrent of obscenities uttered while smoking a cigar. She asked Letterman, whom she referred to as "a sick fuck," if he would sniff her underwear. Despite Letterman's best efforts to avoid addressing the topic, Madonna would not let it go. "I gave him my underpants," she laughed to the audience, "and he won't smell them!" Then, after questioning Letterman about his obsession with her sex life (which was frequently the subject of his comedy monologues), Madonna kept bringing the conversation back to... her sex life.

A ruffled Letterman (showing an uncertain side of himself not frequently seen on television) tried to change the issue in a verbal tug of war, but Madonna was unyielding. "Would you like to touch my dress?" she inquired. Letterman then cut to a commercial. Madonna was smoking a cigar when they returned from the break, stating that it was "just the right size." Later, with the sex chat going nowhere and her double entendre attempts falling flat, she was anxious to be provocative. "Did you know that it's good to pee in the shower?" she inquired, unprompted. The audience was deafeningly quiet. Undaunted, Madonna said, "I'm serious. Peeing in the shower is quite pleasurable. It is effective against the athlete's foot. Urine acts as an antiseptic."

"Don't you know a good pharmacist?" Letterman fired back. "Get yourself some Desenex."

Most observers thought Letterman was expecting to cut Madonna's section short by this point, but Madonna, maybe recognizing she was flailing, wanted to score some points before quitting.

"We have to say good-bye now," Letterman said.

Madonna came to a halt. "She can't be stopped," David declared. "Something's wrong with her!"

"Something is wrong with me," she replied. "I'm sitting here!"

Inexplicably, Madonna resurrected her peeing in the shower craze by proclaiming, "Everybody pees in the shower and picks their noses."

By this point, an audience member was yelling for her to leave the stage, and Letterman was almost pleading with her to do the same, saying that he had other guests on the way. "Thank you for grossing us all out," he muttered to her as she walked away.

"We know that Madonna is not going to appear on a show unless she can make an impact, and on this show she used language to make her impact," says Paul Shaffer, musical director for Letterman's show. I recall thinking to myself, 'The Material Girl has no material.' We were all taken aback, even surprised by it. And it was rather surprising to hear her say such things on national television."

Despite the fact that David Letterman's show was one of his highest-rated, Madonna's participation earned some of the harshest coverage she had ever received. Every report mentioned how she said the word "fuck" thirteen times, causing the network to "bleep" each time. "Alas, it is what the world has now come to expect from Madonna," said Ray Kerrison of the New York Post. She's made a career, if you can call it that, out of blasphemy, lewdness, profanity, and smut. It's a pitiful attempt at stardom and notoriety by a woman who lacks talent and wit. She has nothing except shock to sell. Unfortunately, because she cannot fly with the eagles, she forages with the rodents."

"I called her the next day," her friend Rosie O'Donnell remembers, "and asked her, 'What the heck was all of that about?'" And she was irritated. 'They told me to do it,' she explained. They set everything up. It was basically written, and now they're pretending like they had nothing to do with it."She was quite irritated by that. She stated that she did not want to do it. She stated that she knew better than to do that at this point in her career, but she listened to them. 'People appreciate it when you're surprised,' she was informed. And, against her better judgement, she listened. She admitted that she had made a mistake. She refused to do it. They forced her to do it."

Maybe. Or perhaps not.

Years later, in an interview with Mary Murphy of TV Guide, Madonna admitted, "That was a time in my life when I was extremely angry." I'm angry at the way I was raised. I'm enraged by how sexist the society in which we live is. I was furious with those who assumed that since I was gay, I couldn't be talented. Simply everything. I felt like a victim since the press was continuously picking on me. So I yelled at people, and that night [on Letterman] was one of them. And I'm not particularly pleased with myself."

21. Bedtime Stories

What should she do now? With one scorching issue after another, she had practically ruined her image in recent years. The mostly negative response to Truth or Dare, Sex, Erotica, and Body of Evidence prompted Madonna to consider — finally! — whether she had gone too far, whether she had erected a barrier between herself and her public so high that it would be impossible for her to scale it and reconnect with the world in the way that had always mattered most to her — artistically. The awful performance on David Letterman's show brought home the message. Even when she followed it up with a more subdued appearance on Jay Leno's show, and then another with Letterman at an awards presentation where the two pretended to be great friends, the public was still fed up with her.

According to one of her managers at the time, Madonna understood she needed to make drastic changes in her career or, despite her massive album sales, she would soon be without one. She had always been a wise woman, and while she had obviously slid in recent years, she now recognized that she needed to mature, soften her image, and reconnect with her public. She would endeavour to achieve just that over the following few years... and her album Bedtime Stories would go a long way toward accomplishing that goal.

Bedtime Stories would also be the second of her albums to be issued on Maverick, her own record company, which had been backed with $60 million by Warner Bros. Records (the first was Erotica). Madonna had long desired to release her own music on her own label, and she envisioned the label being a full-service entertainment corporation specialised not just in music but also in television, film, book, and song publishing.

Because Madonna was still a top-selling recording artist in the early 1990s, the presence of her Maverick Records label was unusual. Maverick is more than just a logo for one of the first female musicians to have a genuine label and one of the few women to lead her own entertainment firm. It is a serious endeavour for her, with a staff and executives in place, all of whom were supervised at the time by Freddy DeMann, the company's president. The company's offices were in West Hollywood, in a sleek, inconspicuous single-story office building near one of Madonna's favourite shopping spots, the upscale Fred Segal department store on Melrose Avenue. Madonna and Warren Beatty had explored such a collaboration on various occasions. He had urged her to do it and was claimed to be pleased when she ultimately launched the company.

"My goal, of course, is to have hits with the new company," she added of Maverick. "I'm not one of these stupid artists who is simply given a label to silence her." I requested a record label. So I'm not going to be invisible or just phone in my collaboration. There is no dignity or satisfaction in delegating tasks to others." (Certainly, the most successful artist Madonna has signed to Maverick is Canadian singer/songwriter Alanis Morissette, whose album Jagged Little Pill had sold approximately thirty million copies by the summer of 2000. Cleopatra, the Deftones, Jude, and Prodigy are also on the label.)

The fact that Bedtime Stories would come after the soft erotica of Erotica may have seemed strange to the untrained ear or the casual Madonna fan. After all, even though Bedtime was far gentler in tone than the ethereal-sounding, sexually charged Erotica, it indicated that Madonna, as usual, had a good sense of where pop music was heading at the time of its release. Hip-hop music had totally taken over the national music sales charts by the early 1990s. It was the day's "dance" music, the "new" R&B of a generation of kids dressed in fashionably drooping anti-brand designer jeans and backpacks. It was a trend, and Madonna, predictably, wanted to be a part of it.

Bedtime Stories would go on to become Madonna's most distinctive recording to date. It was her first collaboration with a well-known producer since Nile Rodgers and 1984's Like a Virgin album. (She had opted to deal with relative unknowns on her latest recordings for reasons that were as much about creativity as they were about control.) At this point in her illustrious career, Madonna could have worked with any of the era's top record producers, from Quincy Jones (who'd shepherded Michael Jackson's phenomenal success) to a high-priced journeyman like David Foster (who'd done wonderful work with Barbra Streisand) or Narada Michael Walden (longtime producer of the big-voiced Whitney Houston), or even New Jack Swing producer Teddy Riley.

Madonna sought for the hottest young producers working in urban/hip-hop music for the tracks on Bedtime Stories. Dallas Austin, a twenty-two-year-old songwriter/producer from Atlanta, Georgia, was at the top of her list. He'd gained fame and money creating, among others, male vocal duo Boyz II Men, teen R&B singer Monica, and, most notably, the young female hip-hop trio TLC. Freddy DeMann was also told to contact another well-known personality in pop/R&B, songwriter/producer Kenny "Babyface" Edmonds. Edmonds was the current hitmaker in black music, having written hits for Whitney Houston, Toni Braxton, and other R&B artists.

The inclusion of Austin and Edmonds' names on the CD's producer credits would have demonstrated Madonna's real intent to infiltrate the worlds of R&B and hip-hop. She also added Nellee Hooper to her band of collaborators, who was originally the creative core of a British studio tribe called Soul II Soul, who had 1989 hits with the singles "Keep On Movin'" and "Back to Life (However Do You Want Me)." She also brought on Dave "Jam" Hall, who was then one of urban soul's most reliable rising young songwriter/producers, having scored singles with the R&B girl combo Brownstone, among others. "She knows how to manage a project," Freddy DeMann explains. "She knows how to surround herself with the biggest and best, and I believe that is one of her greatest accomplishments." She is not like many individuals who believe they must do everything themselves. She wants help, but only from the most competent people."

When the first song from Bedtime Stories, "Secret," was released, it stunned both Madonna fans and critics. It's not a big-sounding dance music or a glittering romantic ballad like Madonna's previous work. Instead, it starts with only her voice singing over a rhythmic folky guitar before widening up to a sparse, retro rhythm section. Madonna's distinctive voice remained at the heart of the creation. "My baby's got a secret," she sang, but she never tells the listener what that secret is. She and Dallas Austin penned the ingenious song, which never fails to captivate listeners no matter how many times they hear it. It reached the third spot on the Billboard singles list.

"Take a Bow" was the collection's second single, a sorrowful and masterfully executed ballad written by Madonna and Babyface. "Take a Bow" is a sad, sarcastic all-the-world-is-a-stage ballad about unrequited love (a common motif in Madonna's lyrics) that fooled everyone else but her. "Take a bow," she said, for putting on a magnificent, open show in life and love. (The beautiful video was shot over seven days in Ronda, Spain, with a bullfighting theme (three bulls) and popular bullfighter Emilio Muoz. Alan Parker thought Madonna would be a good fit for the role of Evita in part because of the video's retro feel.)

Though he isn't mentioned as a performer in the credits, Babyface also sings on the single, vocally co-singing Madonna's words in a way that makes their performance sound almost like a duet. It turned out to be a success. "Take a Bow" returned Madonna to the top of the Billboard singles list, where she had become accustomed.

22. Stalked

Madonna, aged thirty-six, was concerned about more than just her public image in the spring of 1995. Although she had become accustomed to being pursued by photographers and fans, she was now being pursued by a fanatic in the form of insane vagabond, twenty-seven-year-old Robert Hoskins. Hoskins had actually convinced himself that he was her husband. In February, he began his quest for Madonna's attention by writing her a distressing series of odd letters signed "Your husband, Bob." He also began abruptly showing up at her house and ringing her security buzzer, possibly seeking to get access to her grounds. Madonna was astonished to discover Hoskins wandering around her land from her bedroom window one morning. She called security, who confined him to the garage for 45 minutes while they waited for the cops.

Madonna fled town, retreating to her new waterfront house in Miami, terrified. Hoskins returned to her property, climbed a twelve-foot fence, and got to within twenty to thirty feet of the home, where he was confronted by security guard Basil Stephens. "I love her!" The security man was yelled at by Hoskins. "I love her, don't you guys understand!"

Hoskins immediately ran at the security guard, yelling for him to move because he was on his way home to visit "his wife." Stephens allegedly shot Hoskins when he attempted to take the security guard's gun.

Madonna was in her Florida home when she learned that her stalker was healing from three bullet wounds in the arm and abdomen at Cedars-Sinai Hospital. Many in the celebrity world were taken aback by the news. She had met Diana, Princess of Wales, at a London party and had asked her to her home. That morning, she learned that Diana wanted to pay her a visit in the near future. "Tell her not to come," Madonna told one of her entourage. "Oh my God, I don't want to be held accountable if anything bad happens to her." Why should she be a part of my worst nightmare?"

"Madonna attracts a lot of crazy people," said Anthony Pellicano, a private investigator in Los Angeles. "Madonna is the worst. She goes out in public and likes to show off."

Madonna was terrified by the stalker's persistence, but she tried to remain calm and carry on with her life and business.

"It really freaked her out," one of her friends stated. "It took a long time for her to accept it. She was terrified of leaving the house. 'When I was younger, I could cope with the crazy out there a lot better,' she said. But as I get older, it becomes more difficult. Maybe I'm losing my cool... or maybe I'm going insane.' She despised her life and career, convinced that she was on the wrong course."

Madonna arrived at her agent's office at CAA (Creative Artists Agency) in Los Angeles unhappy. Her face was pallid and little. Her beautiful crimson lips dominated her appearance. She looked astonishingly slim in a clean white two-piece power trouser suit with matching cap, all straight lines and starch. She complimented her look with a single strand of pearls, matching earrings, and a slender gold watch. She was undoubtedly aware of the looks and murmurs in the waiting room. "Can I assist you?" the receptionist inquired, her voice trembling.

"You want to help me?" Madonna responded abruptly. "Well, we'll see. I require the services of a new agent. This agency is terrible. If you recommend a new agency, you'll be assisting me."

The receptionist was at a loss for words. Madonna grabbed into a silver dish on the secretary's desk and placed a chocolate mint into her mouth, looking irritated. She then dashed into her agent's office, slamming the door behind her.

23. Something to Remember

"There has been so much controversy surrounding my career over the last decade that very little attention is paid to my music." The songs have all but vanished. While I have no regrets about the artistic decisions I've taken, I've come to like the concept of doing things in a more straightforward manner. So, without much fanfare or distraction, I present to you this collection of ballads. Some are old, while others are fresh. "They are all from my heart."

So said Madonna in the liner notes to her eleventh studio album, Something to Remember, released at the end of 1995. Perhaps no more accurate assessment of Madonna or her musical career has ever been provided by the lady herself. Madonna's personal life, like that of so many other powerful female artists from Hollywood's past who have inspired her, has frequently overshadowed her professional achievements. Of course, she forgot to mention that she was generally the source of the distracting insanity. After all, she was the one who had nearly damaged her reputation with her infuriating, one-track-mind sexual outrageousness.

"She knew it was time to make a change," said one of her management team members who requested anonymity. "She'd have to be pretty stupid not to know it, and you'd never accuse Madonna of being stupid." She was concerned and agitated over what others were saying about her. That's why she put together the Something to Remember album, to remind people that she was more than just the controversy that had followed her virtually since her debut."

Madonna was also true when she stated that certain of her songs were frequently missed in favour of current gossip and innuendo. Her talent as a serious pop songwriter has gotten even less notice. For example, the tabloids do not mention that she writes the majority of her songs and releases them through her own Webo Girl Publishing, Inc. "She hasn't shouted about her musical abilities," says

Mirwais Ahmadzai, a rising figure in France's budding electronica scene who produced her 2000 album, Music. "She is the consummate songwriter," he said. "She enjoys classic musicals a lot." Not just the obvious ones, such as Singin' in the Rain, but also the obscure ones. They are adored by her. I recall one occasion when we were all having dinner in Germany and someone mentioned classic musicals, and she was the only one who remembered all the verses. She's interested in everything our parents watch. That's really solid, melodic music. And she writes really good melodic material."

While such details may not make for thrilling headlines, Madonna's involvement in publishing is crucial, especially in an industry where great singer/songwriters create valuable copyrights that they do not own on a daily basis. Madonna is also one of the few hands-on female record producers in the music industry, and one of the most successful of either gender. She can easily compete with legends such as George Martin, the producer of the Beatles (whose chart performances Madonna's hits have challenged), and Quincy Jones.

So, whether Madonna released Something to Remember, a collection of previously released love songs, to establish a point or simply to fulfil a contractual obligation, the fourteen-track album made a statement. That assertion began with the CD packaging. Madonna is dressed to the nines in a form-fitting white cocktail gown. On the front, she is posing in meditation; on the reverse, she is flirtatious, playful, and a little sexual.

According to her notes, not all of the tracks had been re-released; four were brand new. Even though Madonna makes a lot of money when she records a song she wrote, she will willingly and joyfully perform a new song by another writer, or even rework a classic if she feels she can offer something fresh to it. This is the distinguishing characteristic of an artist who is more concerned with the overall project than with how much money she may deposit in her bank account as a result of its sales.

Madonna, a longtime lover of Marvin Gaye's 1976 smash "I Want You," recut the song with the British dance-music group Massive Attack. (It was also included on Motown Records' Inner City Blues — The Music of Marvin Gaye in November 1995.) Nellee Hooper produced the music. Unlike Marvin Gaye's version, which was written by veteran R&B composer Leon Ware and T-Boy Ross (younger brother of Diana Ross), Madonna's rendition is stripped down to simply her voice and Massive Attack's club beat. The end effect is a little sexier than Gaye's rendition; one can almost picture Madonna creeping seductively across the floor, after her prey.

Another new song, "I'll Remember," is the polar opposite of Madonna's take on Gaye. The gorgeous, gold-selling song was written by Madonna, Patrick Leonard, and singer/songwriter Richard Page and served as the theme song for the 1994 film With Honors. It also sounds like a movie theme, complete with clever chords and strong emotion. It's similar to Madonna's second movie theme, "Live to Tell," which is also on the album, but better.

Two new ballads, "You'll See" and "One More Chance," penned by Madonna and songwriter/producer David Foster, were also featured. A star as big as Madonna's working universe is small. She had to work (or consider working) with folks who had success with her peers, even competitors in the pop music business, at some point. Foster has previously produced Barbra Streisand and penned successful songs for Al Jarreau and Earth, Wind & Fire ("After the Love Is Gone"). It was interesting that, with all of his wonderful musical abilities to draw from, he and Madonna would come up with two of the most solemn songs she had ever recorded — but that's the thrill of collaboration: you never know what will come out of it.

The rest of Something to Remember featured some of Madonna's most important ballads, such as "Crazy for You," "Oh Father," "Take a Bow," "Forbidden Love," a remix of "Love Don't Live Here Anymore," "This Used to Be My Playground" (a melancholy performance heard in A League of Their Own and which went on to become her tenth Number 1 record in 1992, making its Madonna album debut here) and "Something to Remember," The fact that she chose the Dick Tracy ballad as the album's title track may show how she felt about the song she and Patrick Leonard wrote, possibly wanting it to get the attention it didn't get the first time around.

In any event, Perhaps all Something to Remember was missing was a bow. It was Madonna's Valentine, a love letter to her followers and music enthusiasts alike. It seemed to say a little more than the obvious, as with any Madonna endeavour. In this example, the collection seemed to nudge her contemporaries teasingly, "...and these are just my ballads."

24. The Stalking Trial

Madonna appeared at a Los Angeles courthouse in a huge black luxury car with tinted windows on Wednesday, January 3, 1996. As the car was driven into an underground garage that is also used to transport prisoners into the building, she could be seen inside wearing dark glasses. Before Madonna was carried into the courthouse by a team of armed bailiffs and bodyguards, reporters were ushered in. Her auburn hair was tied back into a French twist, and she wore a stylish, double-breasted charcoal suit with a calf-length skirt, minimal jewellery, black pumps, and red lipstick. She was gorgeous, yet she appeared frightened.

It was finally time for Madonna to testify in the case against Robert Hoskins, who was accused of stalking and threatening her. She was forced to appear in court under the danger of being incarcerated on $5 million bond because she had previously disobeyed a subpoena to be a witness in the case. She stated from the witness stand that she had not previously appeared because she was terrified of Hoskins and did not want him to see her up close. She went on to tell how his unkempt appearance and "the look in his eye" had bothered her when she passed him one day as he stood in front of the gate at her entranceway. She stated that she grew afraid when Hoskins informed Madonna's assistant (Caresse Norman) that he was Madonna's husband and that he would slice her throat "from ear to ear," then kill Norman and everyone else in the home if he was not permitted to see his "wife." She described having "nightmares that he was in my house, that he was chasing after me."

As her stalker stood just across the room, Madonna, initially clearly scared but then becoming increasingly enraged, expressed her confusion over the judge's decision to order her to appear in the trial. Her attorney, Nicholas DeWitt, had attempted to persuade Judge Jacqueline Connor to allow Madonna to videotape her testimony or, at the very least, to remove Hoskins from the courtroom while she testified. Both motions were denied by the female judge, who stated that Hoskins had a constitutional right to confront his accuser and that she did not want to furnish him with grounds for an appeal. Madonna was taken aback. "She's a woman," Madonna admitted quietly. "Why would she be so spiteful?"

"I'm sick to my stomach," Madonna remarked as she testified. "I feel incredibly disturbed that the man who threatened my life is sitting across from me and he has somehow made his fantasies come true," she explained, her face stern. I'm seated just in front of him. And that's exactly what he wants." During her 75-minute testimony, she avoided making eye contact with Hoskins, just glancing at him twice.

The next day, on January 4, Madonna's bodyguard, Basil Stephens, testified that Hoskins had visited Madonna's Hollywood Hills estate (named Castillo DeLago) three times. Hoskins threatened to kill the bodyguard on his first visit if he did not deliver Madonna a note he had scrawled on a religious pamphlet. Hoskins carried his suitcases with him on his third visit and "looked like he was moving in." Although Hoskins' lawyer argued that he was simply a homeless person, Stephens disagreed, adding that the stalker was "extremely dangerous." The jury was also shown footage from a security camera on the day of the incident as further evidence. It shows Hoskins disobeying a "No Trespassing" sign and climbing the front gate, jumping over a wall onto Madonna's property, and peeping through her front door.

Hoskins' behaviour had escalated from weird to violent during his last visit to Madonna's home in May 1995. During a confrontation, Stephens testified, he was compelled to shoot him. Stephens left the scene to contact the police, believing Hoskins was dead after firing three rounds at him. He returned ten minutes later to find Hoskins sitting up beside Madonna's pool, with wounds to his arm and abdomen. Stephens informed him that an ambulance was on its way.

Stephens recounted telling the devoted fan, "I'm sorry I shot you," in what seemed like a weird scene from a bad movie, to which Hoskins replied, "No problem."

Madonna was so outraged when she learned what had transpired at her home that she chose to sell the $7-million mansion. "How can I lie by the pool knowing this thing happened there?" she asked. I felt attracted to negative energy and knew I had to leave."

After a jury of eight men and four women convicted Robert Hoskins guilty of stalking, the judge sentenced him to ten years in prison, observing that "his apparent mental illness appears to increase the danger."

Following the trial, Madonna continued to have nightmares about Robert Hoskins, who, if he intended to become her obsession, was horrifyingly effective. Madonna stated that she couldn't help but feel that her dreams foreshadowed disaster. She has yet to recover from her encounter with Hoskins. According to those closest to her, she now feels responsible for inciting such a potentially catastrophic event in her life simply by virtue of some of the overtly sexual publicity campaigns (such as the Sex book) she's done in her career, many of which could be perceived as an invitation to harass her by some less emotionally stable people. Growing up, it appears, has not been easy for Madonna, particularly when it comes to recognizing the consequences of her past actions and accepting responsibility for them. Still, as an adult — and especially as a woman who recognized that "each of our actions has a reaction," as she put it — she couldn't disregard the Robert Hoskinses of her life as a byproduct of her popularity. Perhaps he was the unavoidable effect of some of her methods for obtaining popularity.

25. A Race to the Finish

Alan Parker tried not to panic, but after finding that his star actress was expecting a child, he couldn't help but make some quick calculations: how many shooting weeks were remaining on his $59-million project, vs how many more weeks she would appear lean and trim. What else could he say but congratulate Madonna and agree with her that they'd simply have to "see what happens next." They also agreed to keep the pregnancy a secret for fear of disrupting the film due to the media's reaction. Madonna subsequently stated that she felt like a terrified adolescent attempting to conceal an unwelcome pregnancy from her strict parents.

It wasn't long, however, before some of the crew began to question the unexplained and drastic alterations Parker began to make to the filming schedule, particularly with regard to the dance scenes. "They started to wonder if I had finally lost my marbles," Madonna said. As a result, she and Parker were forced to reveal the secret to the other producers. Madonna, on the other hand, kept her pregnancy a secret from her friends and co-stars, knowing that the fewer people who knew about it, the better her chances of keeping it out of the headlines. "I feel like we're all racing against the clock," she stated at the time. "How will I do all those glamorous photo shoots to promote the film when I can't even fit into my costumes?"

Madonna sulked alone in her hotel room at night. Being pregnant should have made her feel better, but it didn't. She had a nagging feeling she was about to damage all she and the crew had fought so hard for. But, she'd think to herself, was success in this film really so important? "All I really want is some peace in my life," she remembered telling no one in particular. "Is that so much to ask?"

The days were long, recording sequences outside in frigid conditions, walking up and down the streets with torch-carrying crowds singing for Perón's freedom. She was on her feet for hours at a time on some days, primarily dancing. As the increasingly unwell Evita, she had to fall to the floor holding her womb in one scene. Madonna painstakingly performed the fall take after take until she was covered in bruises when the scene was eventually completed. Despite her wailing and moaning, she admitted privately that she was really pleased with her performance that day. ("I know it's going to be a very moving scene.") It was all difficult work, probably more so than she had anticipated when she pushed for the position.

When she looked in the mirror at the hotel, she didn't see the joyous glow of pregnancy. Instead, her mirror depicted a tired woman with blemished skin. A network of lines around her mouth and a web of creases around the corners of her eyes were clearly visible. She would begin applying makeup carefully while sitting at her dressing table. Her gaze would not leave her picture until she was certain that her public mask was flawless. However, as she would later recount, it would take her more and longer to reach that goal with each passing day.

Madonna was constantly cold and couldn't seem to warm up. She couldn't even put the day's work behind her so she could relax and, hopefully (but not always), fall asleep. She described herself as feeling terrified and on edge, "like Judy Garland in her final days," to one of her handlers. She'd have to acknowledge later that she couldn't escape the awful feeling that she was witnessing the unravelling of her carefully crafted existence, that all she'd fought so hard to achieve was going to be irreversibly lost.

It wasn't the best of times.

26. No Big Thing?

On April 13, 1996, Madonna's future manager Caresse Norman called America's best gossip writer, Liz Smith — who had always been a great booster of Madonna's career — and verified Madonna's pregnancy. The next day, Smith's piece about it was published in newspapers all across the world. "Surprise, surprise, the stork couldn't wait," wrote Liz Smith. "The happy news from Budapest has just arrived — that Madonna is indeed pregnant."

"Madonna doesn't want this to be a big thing," Liz Rosenberg told Liz Smith in a follow-up call, "though I'm not sure how she thinks it won't be a big deal." But she is deliriously joyful, as is everyone around her. I hate to use cliches, especially when it comes to Madonna, but she is radiant!"

Madonna called her father, Tony, just before the phone call to Liz Smith with the shocking news. During the filming of Evita, she grew closer to her family, ironically through long-distance telephone communication. He was overjoyed every time Madonna called her father from Argentina to let him know how she was doing. He expressed his admiration for her. The various conversations he had with her about her life and job at this time were undoubtedly more courteous than previous conversations. Tony had always appeared to irritate Madonna inadvertently.

For example, a father called daughter a year and a half ago to tell her he had watched the video for "I'll Remember" on television and thought she looked "pretty" in it. Madonna couldn't help but be irritated rather than embrace the compliment.

"But, Dad, it's been out for six months, and you just now saw it?" she recalled telling him.

"Well, we don't watch much television," he went on to say.

"You would think you would keep up with what I'm doing," she said. "My God. "Do you have cable?"

The dispute grew from there. "My father just refuses to acknowledge who I am and what I've accomplished," she later told a reporter.

However, despite being so far away from home and with so much on her mind, Madonna seemed to be able to separate herself from her anguish long enough to feel nostalgic for her father and the rest of her family. "She was homesick," adds her brother Martin, who she also called on a regular basis. "She was calling all of us, her brothers and sisters and even some cousins." "We've been talking, not fighting," Tony informed one relative. "I'm not sure, maybe things are changing." It was almost as if Madonna was converting herself into a softer, more sensible person — the kind of woman she had been trying to persuade her public she was at the time. "Not that she was a saint," adds Parker, "but I did notice that as time went on with the film, she seemed to mellow."

When Madonna found out she was pregnant, she told the press that she didn't want her father to read about it. She called him and told him that he was the most important person in her life — and that she prayed her child would not let her down the way she had let him down so many times before. Of course, Tony was concerned that Madonna was unmarried and didn't appear to be interested in marrying Carlos Leon. Her call, on the other hand, filled him with joy and genuine feeling. "We cried over the phone," he says. "I could see my child was maturing. "And she was nice to me," he laughs. "No smart cracks."

Perhaps her pregnancy finally brought Madonna to terms with the fact that she had only one surviving parent and that she should attempt to be good to him. If she had directed her rage over her mother's death at Tony — and it seemed to most people that she did — perhaps she now recognized how unjust she had been to her father. Perhaps she had just grown to accept her mother's death as a terrible tragedy for which no one was to blame, and that her father's capacity to move on with his own life was an act of strength and courage, rather than a betrayal of her mother's memory. Certainly, if a similar catastrophe befell Madonna, she would continue on with her life, no matter how terrible it would be. The Ciccone spirit is powerful and unwavering, as passed down from father to daughter. Alternatively, the apple doesn't fall far from the tree, as the adage goes.

The expected media frenzy surrounding Madonna's pregnancy came as no surprise to anyone in her group; the news spread as quickly as a war bulletin. Madonna, who has a flair for the dramatic, complained about the attention at work: "Well, the rest of the world knows," she replied at the time. "It's as if my insides have been ripped open." The first page of the Washington Post, CNN, and even Hungarian Radio. "What exactly is the big deal?" She inquired. "I wish everyone would just let me do my work."

Carlos' mother, Maria Leon, 49, a social worker, stepped forward to defend Madonna. "Everything that people say about her is false. When you get to know her, you'll see that she's incredibly affectionate and warm. She, like you and me, is a genuine person." "She loves Carlos very much," his father, Armando, who owns numerous Manhattan check-cashing establishments, remarked. And we adore her." (Armando has stated that when his son first appeared at a family gathering with Madonna for what would subsequently be revealed to be her favourite dinner of black beans, "we couldn't believe it. We assumed it was a doppelganger or something. We spoke and listened to Cuban music all night.")

At this crucial point in the production of Evita, Madonna couldn't help but feel that the public and media attention on her pregnancy was a hindrance. What she actually wanted, she stated, was privacy and peace of mind so she could complete her film.

The jibes at Carlos Leon began almost immediately, making matters more fascinating for the media to report. He had gone to see Madonna in Buenos Aires because she wanted him to be by her side for moral support when she revealed her pregnancy, but he quickly became bored waiting for her while she worked long hours on the shoot. When he returned to New York, he was met with strong media curiosity. "It's great to be back in New York," he grumbled as a photographer shot a photo of him sitting on a seat in Central Park. To his chagrin, the press suddenly referred to him as "Madonna's Top Seed" and her "Baby-Making Beau" (both headlines courtesy of the New York Post).

The press quickly discovered that he was a native New Yorker who grew up on West 91st Street, in a completely different neighbourhood than Madonna's ritzy Central Park co-op (to which he had recently moved). Friends also mentioned Carlos's mild street accent. According to some sources, Carlos anticipated that meeting Madonna would offer him the opportunity for a better life. "Carlos aspired to be more," says an ex-girlfriend who requested anonymity. "He thought maybe he'd get into modelling or acting."

Michael Gacki, a loyal buddy, swiftly came to Carlos's rescue. "He's not riding on her coattails," he told the New York Post. "He gets up at six a.m. every day to work twelve or thirteen hours as a personal trainer to make ends meet." He's been with her for a year and a half, and she hasn't altered him in the least." Gacki went on to say that he and his friend Carlos were both connected with women who were "more successful" than them, but "we both wanted to make sure that we paid our own way."

Patrice Gonzalez, who did not marry Carlos but had a platonic connection with him, today describes Leon as "the kind of guy who can look at people and see them for who they really are, and that includes Madonna." He had a crush on her since they first met. He was surprised that she was as cautious as she turned out to be. "But who knows if he was ever truly in love with her, head over heels? He never wanted to be drawn into her world. She was volatile and tough to be around. He's also a jealous person. He'd be irritated if she complimented a model's appearance in a magazine. They also had disagreements regarding how she handled him from time to time. She's used to directing others."

Gonzalez and Madonna came to see Carlos' parents at their home. As they prepared to depart, Madonna turned to Carlos and stated, very abruptly, "Get my coat."

"Get it yourself," he yelled back at her, his eyes irritably flashing.

"What's the matter with you?" she inquired. "You can't get my coat?"

"Carlos, go get her coat," his mother, Maria, urged, trying to maintain order. "Be a gentleman."

"Look, I'm not your personal assistant," Carlos said, dismissing his mother's request. Most onlookers concluded that Carlos was concerned with more than just retrieving his girlfriend's coat. Perhaps he and Madonna had previously discussed similar subjects. "If you want me to get your coat, say 'please'," he instructed. "I am not employed by you. "You know, I'm not on the payroll."

Madonna gave him a chilly look as she rolled her eyes. "My God," she grumbled.

"Oh, now I understand," Carlos exclaimed. "You see, I had completely underestimated your capacity for being . . . bitchy."

Madonna appeared irritated, but she managed to keep her cool. She acquiesced, perhaps to soften the blow because Carlos's mother was watching. "Carlos, can I ask you to get my coat?" she asked, softly adding, "Por favour."

"Now, now," his mother remarked as Carlos assisted Madonna with her coat. See how lovely it is?"

According to Patrice Gonzalez, when Madonna eventually told Carlos she was pregnant, he recognized that this child would create a link with her that he would have for the rest of his life. "This was a big adjustment for him," Gonzalez said, "and forced him to look at her another way, as a woman who would be in his life for the long run."

Many reporters speculated that Madonna was carrying the baby as a kind of outrageous publicity stunt for her film. Though she was upset, she shouldn't have been startled by the implication. After all, she appeared to many observers to be willing to go to any length to promote a project. So why not try this? "People have suggested that I have done this [become pregnant] for shock value," she went on to say. "These are remarks that only a man would make." It is far too tough to be pregnant and bring a child into the world for frivolous or provocative reasons. "There are also rumours that I used my father as a stud," she stated. "This implies that I am incapable of having a genuine relationship." I realise these are all remarks from people who can't bear the thought that something positive is happening to me. They can't ruin something special and wonderful."

27. Betrayal

Madonna was well aware of the pitfalls of her global celebrity. It had undoubtedly cost her privacy, but she was used to dealing with that fact. She also realised that she had made some serious romantic mistakes in her life. She vowed to be more selective after Tony Ward. She was, however, a sexual creature with normal needs and desires. She didn't want to commit to a serious relationship with the wrong man, but she did want to share physical intimacy with someone. Anyone who knew her could understand why she would become intimately involved with libidinous basketball star Dennis Rodman. A bad choice, however, is still a bad choice, even if it results in mind-blowing sex... Dennis ended up betraying their relationship by discussing it in his memoir Bad As I Wanna Be.

Madonna began dating Dennis Rodman, a basketball player two years her junior who had an eccentric reputation — on and off the court — two years earlier, in 1994, before the filming of Evita. He relished the celebrity spotlight as much as Madonna did, with his outlandish appearance — bleached blond hair, tattoos, and various piercings — and flamboyant behaviour. In fact, he frequently made controversial moves for the sake of titillation, such as the time he announced his wedding and then showed up at the resulting press conference in full drag, complete with wedding gown and veil. He then announced his intention to marry himself.

The games started when Madonna first met Dennis and asked for his phone number. He gave her his fax number instead of his phone number. "You're trying to fuck with me," she faxed him the following day. "You gave me a number for your cursed machine. "What's the matter?"

But it wasn't long before playful and sometimes sexy love messages were being exchanged between the two. "I want to have six kids," Rodman faxed to Madonna, "what do you think?"

She faxed back to Rodman that six children were fine with her, but they needed to get to work right away. "You think I'm joking, but you'll see that I'm not," she wrote in an email. She also stated that even if Dennis was broke and working at a car dealership, she would still be interested in him. "Lay in your bed, close your eyes and fuck me at some point today," she went on to say.

Dennis Rodman, perhaps because he was at the peak of his own fame, seemed unimpressed by Madonna's fame or wealth, which only served to make him more appealing in her eyes. Dennis' pal recalls attending a party with Rodman and Madonna. "He and I were flirting with some girls," he said. "Madonna kept trying to interrupt, but he just ignored her." When Rodman eventually gave Madonna his phone number (not his fax number, finally), she launched a campaign to win him over. "She called ten to fifteen times a day," claims Rodman's pal. "She kept asking him, 'What's up?'" 'What are you up to?'"

Dennis told pals in early 1995 that Madonna was "a lot of fun." Meanwhile, Madonna told her confidantes that she loved Dennis, though it's hard to picture any of them believing it — or that she believed it herself. It's more likely that she was carried away by their sexual chemistry. When he was unavailable and she couldn't contact him on the phone (perhaps because he was filtering his calls?), she swamped him with amorous faxes with salutations like "Good morning, Daddy Long Legs."

These ridiculous games and pleasure lasted only a few months and resulted in little more than a wild journey in the bedroom for both parties. Madonna cancelled the relationship after discovering Dennis speaking about her to common friends. Later, when some of her faxes to him were published in the tabloid the Globe, she understood that, if anything, she had been unfortunate in passion. Rodman's comments to Playboy that he had to terminate it with her when she began pressuring him to conceive her — a recurring theme in her life at the time with the men she dated — enraged her even more. (According to Rodman, "she said, 'Be in a hotel room in Las Vegas on this specific day so you can get me pregnant.'" He refused.)

Rodman wrote his autobiography a little more than a year later. He was open about his and Madonna's foreplay and pillow conversation in it: "She wasn't an acrobat. She wasn't a dead fish, but she wasn't alive either." When the memoir was out, Madonna dashed to the bookstore and bought a copy for herself. According to accounts, she became so enraged after reading the chapter about her that she flung the book into the flames.

"A certain disgusting basketball player I made the mistake of going out with decided to publish an autobiography and devoted a whole chapter to what it was like to have sex with me," Madonna said in a statement. "Complete with made-up dialogue that not even a bad pornographer would take credit for." It's so ridiculous that I'm sure no one will take it seriously, but I don't want to read the headlines, and of course, I feel exploited once more by someone I trusted and let into my life."

She further stated, "When I first knew him, I sent him a few very silly faxes with really childish drawings on them, and months after I'd stopped seeing him, they appeared on [the tabloid TV program] Hard Copy, and I thought, "This is merely the beginning . . ."

Madonna's fans may be astonished to learn that she was too private to reveal the truth about her connection with Rodman, which, as it turned out, bore little resemblance to the way he depicted it in his book. According to personal acquaintances of Madonna and Rodman, the couple only participated in sexual activity twice — not the "fifty to a hundred times" Rodman boasted about in his book.

"He told me very specifically that he and Madonna had slept together one time in Miami, and that it was a big disappointment," says dancer Trina Graves, who dated Rodman in Chicago. He blamed it on her, claiming she was cold. He claimed he couldn't feel thrilled around her because she was too demanding in bed. He claimed she emasculated him.

"However, after spending time with Dennis, I can see the other side." He's far too self-centred to make love to a woman in a way that would be remembered. My time with him was dull and monotonous. Nothing noteworthy." Graves recalls the basketball star not even taking off his silk suit for their meeting. Rather than a lovemaking session, he simply dropped his pants in a way that implied a pornographic moment. "And, no," she said, "he did not become aroused with me, either."

"Madonna made a vow a long time ago to only have sex with a man once if he proved himself too selfish to care about her satisfaction — and that certainly defines Dennis's approach," says a friend of Madonna's who has known her for twenty years. She also desired more from a man than Dennis could provide. She was assured of it."

Madonna told this particular acquaintance that she and Dennis got drunk one night and fell into bed together. "The poor guy couldn't even get excited for her," a buddy commented. "That night, she blamed it on the alcohol." The following night, she broke her rule and let him try again.

"Dennis delivered this time, but only to his satisfaction, not hers. The entire thing took roughly fifteen minutes. That was the end of it. They never slept together again."

According to a friend of Madonna's, once Dennis' book was published, she opted not to reveal the truth about her affair with him because she didn't want to "be as mean to him as he'd been to her, lying about her in his book." Nothing was true." Despite her claims to the public that the book was "full of lies," Madonna chose to let

Rodman have his macho image. She didn't say anything about him being a flop in the bedroom. "Madonna could have put a dent in Rodman's machismo reputation if she had decided to tell the truth about his sexual prowess," says the insider, "but I guess she chose to have mercy on him." "She said, 'I feel sorry for the creep.'"

During Madonna's appearance with Oprah Winfrey, Oprah mentioned that she had read in the news that Rodman wanted to apologise to Madonna for the book (which had spent eight weeks at the top of the New York Times best-seller list and had certainly gotten him a lot of publicity). "Well, he'd better crawl from here to China," Madonna remarked. In fact, Madonna and Dennis had previously discussed the book over the phone. Rodman was able to call Madonna in London and apologise "for any misunderstandings."

According to reports, she told him, "Dennis, you and I both know what happened when we made love... and it was nothing to write a book about."

28. Role Model?

Because she is so widely renowned for her public relations skills, it should come as no surprise that Madonna enjoys giving media interviews. Despite the fact that she believes she has said everything she wants to say to the press — and more than once — she recognizes the significance of publicity and is always willing to play the game if it is essential in her life and work. She despises most reporters and writers, calling them "parasites!" but admits that dealing with them is a necessary evil. Even though she was weary by her schedule while filming Evita, she understood she had to connect with the press. After all, she was filming a high-budget film with a lot riding on it, not just for her but also for the film's producers. She recognized that any publicity would definitely improve the situation. Still, she couldn't help but be wary of the media, owing to the way her pregnancy was portrayed in the news.

Madonna was hurt, even enraged, to read newspaper editorials arguing whether she was a good role model for young females. Madonna screamed angrily to a reporter that society is "sick." When pushed to elaborate, she said, "This strange interest and fascination with... well, you'd think I was the first celebrity who wasn't married to get pregnant." The amount of attention and how biassed it is is simply insane. What I'm doing seems so strange."

She was especially enraged to learn that Camille Paglia, the renowned gay feminist, had indicated that Madonna was having an unwed kid because she was unable to bond with a man. Paglia stated that the public has reason to be concerned about the child's well-being. "Does anyone complain that neither Susan Sarandon nor Goldie Hawn is married to the father of her children?" Madonna replied by slamming her palm against a table. When Woody Allen and Mia Farrow had a kid and continued to live across the park from each other, no one said anything. "Why aren't these people held up as role models?"

Madonna believed — possibly correctly — that the public would feel more at ease if she just married Carlos Leon, only for the marriage to fail. But, in order to be honest about her future with Leon, she had to confess that there was none. She was not about to enter into a marriage with him only to appease the public.

"I don't want to be a spokesperson for marriage, OK?" she raged to a reporter for the news magazine USA Weekend. "I should be able to pick and choose what I want to be a spokesperson for." Why can't I advocate for free expression, safe sex, and other similar causes? That is freedom of expression: "I don't feel like I have to get married to have a good relationship and raise healthy children."

Perhaps the wisest course of action would have been to simply halt the frenzy... to stop doing interviews, reading stories about herself, and calling reporters to discuss what they had written. However, she couldn't stop herself. "If she knew something was going to be published, she had to read it," one of her former colleagues claimed. "And, oh my God!" she had to argue over it. One would think she'd have enough on her mind with the film, but not Madonna. She also had to deal with the media. Why? "I'm not sure..."

Perhaps the reason for Madonna's press conduct is that, as evidenced by her previous behaviour, she appears to be a person who needs as much drama in her life as possible. She seemed impelled to discover a justification for mayhem when it becomes too calm. She appears to have to find a justification for chaos when she feels she has finally focused on a project. Madonna is the name.

With only two weeks left of filming, the pregnant actress was understandably fatigued. For five months, she had gotten up at six a.m. every day to undergo three hours of fussing and style, her hair whipped into the ornate braids and rolls of the 1940s. Her nails were expensively manicured, her eye colour was changed to brown with unpleasant and annoying contact lenses, and fake teeth were awkwardly placed. Madonna felt as if she had put in a full day before even starting work. Despite her efforts to focus her vision as she stepped onto the scene in full costume, her surroundings were frequently a blur. Madonna performed those last few weeks in a dissatisfied manner, as set designers and customers looked on with approval.

At the same time, she felt guilty about any attention she could offer to the movie. She later admitted that she frequently found herself "apologising to my unborn child for any uncomfortable bouncing around I was causing." She wanted to go shopping for baby gear, but she knew she'd have to wait two weeks until the movie was finished before succumbing to the call of parenthood.

Ironically, some of the film's most demanding scenes were scheduled for the last two weeks. In the latter weeks of production, she was called to do Eva's exhausting dying scenes, as well as close-up retakes of the dramatic balcony scene. To prepare herself for the horror ahead, she put some aspirins into her mouth and rapidly gulped them with some Evian water. She did what she knew she had to do after casting a scared glance in Alan Parker's way. "The intensity of the scenes we've been shooting and the amount of emotional work and concentration needed to get through the day are so mentally and physically exhausting that I'm sure I will need to be institutionalised when it is over," she wrote in the Vanity Fair "diary."

Throughout it all, the one thing that kept Madonna going was the same thing that had always kept her going: the desire to achieve greater success than she had previously known. Her instincts told her she was doing her greatest job in this film. More than being a music sensation or a great concert singer, she had always wished to be a movie star. Despite this, it had always seemed the most elusive objective. If she could simply hang on and keep doing the best work she could with the kind of quality performance she'd been providing since the start of work on Evita, Madonna was confident that her future in movies would be secure. That kind of achievement would undoubtedly make all of her trials and tribulations worthwhile. At least, that's what she assumed at the time.

29. Anticlimax

The final day of filming Evita, on May 27, 1996, proved to be an anticlimax for Madonna after all of her hard work, worry, and expectation. She would later acknowledge that she had fantasised of an emotional conclusion to her journey. She saw herself sobbing in front of her coworkers after saying her final lines because she was absolutely overwhelmed by the experience. While she would be relieved that the job was over, she would equally be sorry that it was time to say goodbye to all of those great individuals she had grown to love and admire, and who had shown her such love and admiration in return — or so she imagined. Madonna had even gone to the bother of rehearsing a dramatic, sad farewell speech, one that each crew member and co-star would take home with them as part of their pleasant memories of her, one that they would be able to recount to family and friends... and maybe even future Madonna biographers. Running a shaky palm over her brow, she was almost ready to deliver her remarks in regal, Evita manner when, at the end of the last shot, Alan Parker said, "That's a wrap." However, before she could finish her address, everyone dispersed and immediately went about the task of breaking down the sets. Nobody gave her a second glance.

It was all over in an instant. However, as Madonna later acknowledged, she did not feel the way she expected to feel. As she later recalled, there was no sadness, elation, or appreciation. Rather, she simply felt... numb. She blinked, her eyes welling up with tears. Then she gazed around helplessly, as if attempting to make sense of what had just transpired. Perhaps observing her bewilderment, someone approached her, hugged her heartily, and then murmured something — she can't remember what — in her ear.

There were no speeches or tearful goodbyes as the crew packed away its belongings. "I was just too damn tired," Madonna explained afterward. "And so was everyone else."

There had been a total of 299 scenes. Four thousand extras dressed in mediaeval attire appeared. Nearly 6,000 outfits from twenty different costume houses in London, Rome, Paris, New York, Los Angeles, and San Francisco were required. Madonna's wardrobe included 85 distinct outfits, 39 hats, 45 pairs of shoes, 56 pairs of earrings, and as many different hairstyles as there were hairstyles – while the art department built 320 separate sets, comprising 24,000 accessories.

Madonna's filming stopped barely in time, because not only was her stomach pressing against her tailored outfits, but she was also on the verge of an emotional breakdown. "I couldn't have taken one more minute of it," she'd say later.

Despite the fact that she had completed the film, the pregnant actress was not given much time to rest. Disney Studios' advertising machine kicked into high gear in order to sell Evita to the audience. The company was eager to make the film's release an "event" by announcing early bookings and "exclusive-run" debuts in big American cities. Within weeks of her return to the United States, Madonna found herself at the centre of a huge campaign that featured advertising in fashion publications to promote the "Evita look." Vanity Fair, for example, enabled her to publish what would turn out to be one of the world's longest press releases in its November 1996 issue, something called "Madonna's Private Diaries."

"This is a diary of sorts," Madonna wrote in an introduction to the lengthy documentary, "a sketchbook of feelings, ideas, and dreams, all relating to one subject — the making of Evita... the month before shooting began, I made a promise to myself that I would write down everything that happened to me." I got butterflies in my stomach and knew I was in for a wild journey. "I was determined to remember every detail." Madonna's fans devoured this meal, as they did everything she served, failing to notice that persons who keep "private diaries" to capture crucial events in their lives don't normally publish them in international magazines some months later. However, Madonna's "sketchbook" of emotions did provide some important background material on the creation of the film, which, as intended, piqued the reader's interest in seeing it.

Madonna had been significantly affected by her pregnancy by September 1996. On September 9, she began keeping a pregnancy journal. She said in it that there were days when she couldn't even function since her mood swings made life tough for her. She also mentioned haemorrhoids and back issues, saying, "My life has been hell."

She did, however, have some fun with her buddies. "Once she finished Evita, we got to spend a lot of time together," Juliette Hohnen, her close friend, explains. "It was probably the first time in years she was forced to stay in one place for an extended period of time." We laughed as we practised our runs from her house to the hospital in preparation for the big day. We always made a mistake turning someplace, no matter how many times we practised, and then, like a couple of fighting sisters, we blamed each other for lousy driving or bad navigation."

Madonna kept a video diary of her pregnancy in addition to a written record. Friends who have watched her video history feel it is so moving that it should be made public. According to a source, "She spoke about how difficult the pregnancy was, how sick she became, how her face became blemished, how unattractive she felt, and how she knew it would all be worth it for her child." I'm confident that when her daughter watches these movies in the future, she will experience a special closeness to her mother that Madonna never felt with hers — which was one of Madonna's aspirations with this project."

"M [many of her friends call her "M"] told me that feeling a baby growing within her made her want to make an effort to straighten out some of the things she'd done in the past that she wasn't happy about now," said her good friend. "For instance, I know that during her pregnancy she at least attempted to mend her years-long rift with Michael Jackson."

Michael hadn't spoken to Madonna since he cancelled the video in which Madonna had wanted Michael to dress as a woman. However, in the fall of 1996, Madonna sent Michael a note wishing him luck on the start of a tour he was embarking on at the time, as well as a massive flower arrangement to Prague, where he opened his act. It was difficult for her to stop from making harsh remarks about him.

"She also began calling people she hadn't talked to or seen in years," adds her buddy. "She told me she wanted to be a good mother but was afraid she wouldn't be able to because she had become so accustomed to being a self-centred person," Diane Giordano said. She grew spiritual and began to see herself in a new and uncompromising light. So M's pregnancy was an emotional and very human time for her — and for everyone in her life who received unexpected, late-night phone calls from Madonna pleading for forgiveness. Being pregnant and carrying the child to term was the most difficult thing she'd ever had to do, more difficult than anything she'd done in her job. Being pregnant, as it is for many women, was a watershed moment in her life."

Despite how difficult it was, especially at the end of her pregnancy, she tried to enjoy her leisure time. Recalls Julia Hohnen, "When she was nine months pregnant, we decided to go to an art exhibition." We had to lie down in the back of a filthy minivan to evade the ever-present photographers. So much for opulent transportation."

She also tried to attend as many parties as she could in order to keep herself busy. In September 1996, at a gathering for photographer

Herb Ritts at Perino's restaurant in Beverly Hills, a very pregnant Madonna (wearing a powder-blue cut-on-the-bias dress designed by Susan Becker, a simple matching sweater by Anna Molinari, and the diamond-studded gold watch Donatella Versace gave her for her birthday) admitted to close friends that she felt out of place, "fat and ugly and just awful." She was standing in the corner, alone and depressed. Ritts passed right past her, not noticing her, and when he did spot her, he apologised and said, "I'm sorry I missed you." "I don't see how anyone could miss me," she remarked. "I'm the size of a fucking house."

She had peculiar cravings: poached eggs and omelettes of all kinds, caramel and strawberry ice cream, pizza, cheeseburgers, and other junk foods. One witness described her as standing in a corner of a small grocery shop in a seedy neighbourhood of Hollywood, "eating one of those awful hot dogs with a soft drink."

30. Ray of Light

By 1998, Madonna, then 39, had nearly completed what was possibly her most ambitious makeover in her fifteen-year career. For the last few years, she had been busy repairing the public relations damage caused by sexually explicit projects in four different media: Truth or Dare in video, Sex in publishing, Erotica in music, and Body of Evidence in film. Madonna had wisely chosen to transition from her reputation as a sexual rebel to a more restrained persona as a mother and New Age thinker.

But it was more than simply public relations. Her encounters with Evita and her new baby, Lourdes, had had a profound effect on her. "It's just an evolution, really, since I made Evita," she told Gerri Hirshey of Rolling Stone. "Because I went down to South America and got beaten up in the way that I was in the newspapers every day — and sort of living vicariously through what happened to Eva Perón — and then I got pregnant." Going from the depths of despair to the other side... you know, becoming a mother has given me a whole new perspective on life. I see the world as a much brighter place now. "I just have an endless amount of compassion for other people."

Ray of Light, her first album published following the birth of her daughter, was released in March 1998. It would blend her newly adopted New Age ideals — which she seemed to have fine-tuned with Andy Bird's assistance — with music that was both current and trendsetting. Ray of Light was, without a doubt, a recording that demonstrated without a doubt that Madonna still knew how to stay ahead of the game in mainstream music.

Madonna realised that at her core, despite the movies, soundtracks, and poignant songs, she was still a dance music artist. She also knew that trends in that genre begin in locations where people dance, which is where Madonna's new sound will emerge.

For years, techno and electronica had been the music played at raves, enormously popular, illegal underground parties held in abandoned warehouses and empty regions on the outskirts of town all over the world. This is where teenage music fans zoning out to the pulse of such airy, synthesised sounds, high on booze and the popular rave drug Ecstasy. It was a scorching sound that Madonna was well aware had not reached the public. "It's definitely an area that's gone untapped," Madonna said at the time. "And I need to be in on it."

Madonna wisely realised that in order to make an authentic album of techno-pop, she'd need to go to the source of such music, just as she had sought out the hot dance/pop producer of the moment to assist her foray into mainstream success (Nile Rodgers with Like a Virgin) and employed hot, urban producers to accommodate her hip-hop move (Dallas Austin with Bedtime Stories). She had planned to work with Robert Miles, Trent Reznor, Nellee Hooper, Babyface, and William Orbit at first. Only Orbit — a known writer and producer in the realm of techno and electronica — was kept in the end, most likely in an attempt to give the project a solid character. (According to Madonna historian Bruce Baron, there may have been early demos of Ray of Light songs co-produced with one or more of the original lineup. He claims that none have been discovered thus far.)

While William Orbit brought his team of collaborators, Madonna once again leaned on the stalwart Patrick Leonard. Leonard would anchor Orbit's technology musically and, as he described it, "keep the resulting album sounding like it was Madonna at its core." He explains, "She didn't want to lose her identity." "She just wanted to expand her sound." This group would work together to create what may be considered Madonna's most ambitious undertaking since the musically complex Evita.

Madonna did not invent anything new with Ray of Light. Madonna merely adapted the core of the techno scene — its sound and personality — to the commercial dance music sensibility she'd come to master. Like the Beatles in the sixties, who went from the goofy and melodic "She Loves You" to the psychedelia madness of "Lucy in the Sky with Diamonds" in a matter of years, Madonna simply did what she knew she had to do to stay current: she brilliantly "morphed" into the current trend. She just happens to be able to stay up with the times better than most of her contemporaries, many of whose attempts to keep up with the musical times sound unbelievably manufactured.

The album's first single, "Frozen," is a simple yet majestic song about spiritual growth in someone who doesn't seem to want it, made attractive by captivating vocal melodies and Moroccan musical nuances. The song was a huge success, reaching number two on the Billboard singles chart.

"Ray of Light," the album's title tune and second hit, embodied everything Madonna hoped to achieve with the project. The tune opens with a peaceful, melodic guitar sound before transitioning to a determined beat and whirlwinding artificial sound. Lyrically, it's a celebration of power and self-expression. Her abandon is infectious, as the track sweeps the listener away. The song was an instant hit, debuting at No. 5 on the Billboard charts - her greatest chart position to date. (Previously, in December 1995, "You'll See" debuted at Number 8 and, in March 1998, "Frozen" equaled that entry position.). "Ray of Light," Madonna's forty-first chart song and thirty-second Top 10 smash, reflected the high feeling of the time — the "new" spirit of the millennium.

The song "The Power of Good-bye," about the strength that comes from letting go, has a pleasant Europop flavour to it. Indeed, Ray of Light contains lyrical reflections about the person Madonna believes she used to be and who she has become. For example, in "Nothing Really Matters," she admits to her selfish behaviour in the past.

"I don't really want to dissect my creative process too much," she remarked when asked to describe the songs she writes by reporter Jancee Dunn. "Really, what's the point?" I want people to react viscerally and emotionally to things, rather than wondering where all this stuff came from. I don't want people to think about their relationship and then think about my bug crawling across the floor if I see a bug crawling across the floor and that inspires me to create the most wonderful love poetry."

Without a single reference to bondage or oral sex in a single lyric, the songs on this album instead spoke of ecology, the universe, the earth, "the stars in the sky," angels and heaven, and, to the surprise of some onlookers, contained polite references to God and "the Gospel." In one song, she speaks of "waiting for the time when the earth shall be as one," while in another, she attempts to construct a pop dance song out of a yoga chant. However, when the album was released, the music business as a whole, despite being unwaveringly supportive of an artist as commercially successful as Madonna, did not believe it would be a hit. Some critics claimed that the tracks' sound was not radio-friendly. Other critics argued that Madonna was too old for this type of record, at least by pop music standards. They were all incorrect. Ray of Light went on to sell four million copies in the United States and twelve million worldwide. It also introduced an older pop icon to younger fans as an artist to whom they could relate and embrace musically.

Madonna, who was nearly forty years old at the time, had also introduced a new physical image that included the use of togas and saris, as well as veils over long, flowing dark tresses. Her come-hither looks were gone, as were her panties worn as outerwear. She was shot with a reflecting smile on her face and divine winds blowing through her hair. Her face was altered to have the bronzed, perfect complexion that one might expect to see only on an angel. Nonetheless, Madonna was vehemently opposed to the impression that she was always changing herself. "I'd rather think that I'm slowly revealing myself, my true nature," she went on to say. "It feels to me like I'm just getting closer to the core of who I really am."

With Ray of Light's critical acclaim and financial success, Madonna's image shift proved to be yet another achievement. Surprisingly, throughout her fifteen years of stardom, she had only gotten one Grammy, for Best Video in 1991. (It's not uncommon for acclaimed performers to never win a Grammy. Madonna was in good company, including the Beatles and Diana Ross, among others.) With a new career and image, Madonna won four Grammys at the Los Angeles ceremony at the Shrine Auditorium in February 1999 (during which she performed "Nothing Really Matters" in a dazzling red kimono, oriental-style makeup, and straight black hair) — Best Pop Album, Best Dance Recording, Best Short Form Music Video, and Best Record Packaging. (The following year, at the Grammys, Madonna added another trophy to her collection when she was named Best Song.) "Beautiful Stranger" was written for the film Austin Powers: The Spy Who Shagged Me.

Although Ray of Light and the newer, more mature Madonna were highly accepted, her plans for a tour were put on hold while she focused on her film career. In 1998, she was on the verge of signing a deal to co-star with Goldie Hawn in a high-budget film adaptation of the Broadway musical Chicago (which never materialised), and she had already signed on to star in The Next Best Thing, a romantic comedy starring Rupert Everett, fresh off his smash success in My Best Friend's Wedding, a commercially successful Julia Roberts vehicle. The revised script, which Everett brought to Madonna's attention, pushed My Best Friend's Wedding's secondary story — a straight woman/gay guy friendship — to the foreground. The two friends in The Next Best Thing had one night of inebriated intimacy and then decide to accept the subsequent pregnancy and raise the child together.

But, once again, Madonna's film career would be less than

illustrious. When The Next Best Thing was finally released (on March 3, 2000), it was met with the same venom as anything she had ever done before. The New York Post remarked, under the banner "Her Best Is Bad," that "there hasn't been a movie as smug or cheesy as The Next Best Thing in quite a while." It then went on to complain, "For the first half of the movie, Madonna speaks with an unexplained English accent that draws attention to the singer's apparent inability to read a line." In its analysis, USA Today would be more succinct: "Madonna still can't act." (She would have a smash single with "American Pie," a version of the 1971 Don McLean pop classic recorded by Madonna for The Next Best Thing.)

"I think half of my movies have been good, and the other half have been shit," she has stated of her cinematic career. "I have two things going against me. One reason is that I'm quite successful in another area, and it's really difficult for people to let you cross over into anything else. Also, because I was in a string of awful movies, it gave people the right to say, "Oh, she can't act." She is incapable of doing this or that.' But, to be honest, I can think of Academy Award winners who have done more bad movies than I have."

31. Madonna's Moment

She had grown as a person, not just as a mother, but also as a girlfriend. By the end of 1999, it appeared that Madonna's parental achievements had also changed the way she reacted to the guy in her life. She was more patient or, at the very least, tried to be empathetic after dealing with her child's requests. Of course, it was impossible for her not to act confidently on occasion. After all, she was still a wealthy woman who had spent the better part of the previous fifteen years as a spoiled, self-involved celebrity. However, she was now aiming to be a more well-rounded, giving person, not only because of Lourdes, but also because of all of those previous horrible romances. "I finally figured out that if you want to have the right kind of man in your life, you have to be the right kind of woman," she told Cosmopolitan. Madonna's connection with Guy Ritchie was functioning in ways that men like Sean, Warren, John Jr., or even Carlos and Andy simply could not.

Guy enjoyed it when Madonna talked about his projects rather than just her own. It made him happy to see her with Lourdes, whether she was playing with her, punishing her, or simply having a quiet moment. She wasn't as selfish as she had been in the past, but he had never known that side of her. As difficult as it may have been for her opponents to accept — or even believe — "the Material Girl" had matured into the kind of woman a man may want not only in his life, but in the life of his child. Certainly, being Madonna's consort came with a lot of emotional baggage — there were days when she could be tough, demanding, and unreasonable — but Guy appeared to think it was worth it, especially when he was at home, alone with the woman he loved to call "the missus."

Guy and Madonna appear to the outside world to be an exceptionally attractive pair, tanned and healthy, lithe and smiling, with the unassuming aura of two who have the finest life has to give. Despite their best efforts to understand each other, their petty disputes and conflicts are typical of any normal marriage... but in unusual circumstances. Guy, for example, found himself in the centre of a classic Madonna-related drama at the end of December 1999, when the couple spent New Year's Eve at Donatella Versace's Miami Beach estate.

Madonna requested — and received — a police escort to the Versace bash so she wouldn't have to fight traffic getting past the millenium crowds cramming the twelve-bedroom, thirteen-bathroom Ocean Drive mansion where Gianni Versace was murdered in July 1997.

"Seemed a little extreme to me," Guy remarked later in front of the partygoers. He looked great in the kind of "couture" pinstriped suit that certain English gentlemen prefer.

"Well, I absolutely despise traffic," Madonna stated, pouting. She then removed her shawl and handed it to Guy without saying anything. She wore a pinch-waisted shirt and a fitted skirt inspired by the 1940s below.

"But you weren't even driving," Guy pointed out as he accepted the robe. "We were in a limousine."

"And your point is?" Madonna questioned, looking at him.

"My point is—" Guy started to explain. He seemed obstinate in his refusal to drop the matter.

"Oh my goodness. Guy! "Please," Madonna exclaimed, smiling. She then took Gwyneth Paltrow's hand in hers and began strolling with her into a crowd. (Gwyneth and her lover Guy Oseary, the CEO of Madonna's Maverick label, were staying in Madonna's guest house in Coconut Grove, Miami Beach.) "He has a lot to learn about dating a woman of means," Madonna stated of Guy, her accusation softened by a sly smirk. Gwyneth, dressed in skinny suede leggings and a belted leather jacket, smiled and waved an index finger at her buddy, as if to say, "Now, now. Don't be unconvertible."

"A double Scotch," Guy said to the hovering waiter. He laughed and shook his head. "No rocks."

Madonna and Guy Ritchie were joined by Gwyneth Paltrow, Guy Oseary, Ingrid Casares, Rupert Everett, Madonna's brother Christopher Ciccone, and Orlando Pita, her hairdresser, at the dinner for 75 in the mansion's patio. As semi-clad guys served hors d'oeuvres and champagne, giant plastic tarpaulins were hung to palm trees on either side of the home to conceal the view of any admirers or photographers.

"It was a true night of decadence and debauchery," Madonna recalled later. "It was the best New Year's Eve I've ever spent." There were shirtless males with oiled bodies dancing on podiums, a mambo band playing, and incredibly good food. People were leaping up and down on the furniture and pogoing. I'm not sure how many cocktails I had. All I know is that they kept gushing out of the glass, and before you knew it, you had twenty half-drinks... I had the best bunch of pals."

As Madonna and her guests were finishing their steak and salmon, actress/singer Jennifer Lopez walked in uninvited. Jennifer was in Miami to avoid the spotlight in New York after her recent arrest with her boyfriend Sean (Puffy) Combs. As soon as Madonna observed Jennifer, a dark vibe appeared to envelope her – she was a little tipsy by this point. She stood up and told her pals, "Dinner's over." She then proceeded to a distant area of the patio, accompanied by four of her five companions: the two Guys (Ritchie and Oseary), Ingrid, and Rupert. Gwyneth, on the other hand, remained at the table, gazing earnestly into an empty wine glass and appearing to be lost in concentration.

Gwyneth had had a rough New Year's Eve, having recently opted to break her brief romance with Guy Oseary, explaining that he "just isn't right for me." She did, however, pledge to uphold a commitment she made to him to be his date for the all-important New Year's Eve.

Earlier in the day, Madonna and her pals boarded her yacht and set off from her property's wharf, bound for Rosie O'Donnell's Miami house in South Beach, which is about fifteen minutes away by boat. Madonna's bodyguard piloted the yacht. Gwyneth spent nearly an hour at O'Donnell's crying on Madonna's shoulder about how much she missed actor and former boyfriend Ben Affleck, whom she met on the set of Shakespeare in Love in 1997 (for which she received an Academy Award). Perhaps because she was caught in the middle of a difficult position — Guy Oseary was not only her business partner at Maverick, but also a close friend — Madonna tried to be diplomatic and understanding. She shortened her visit to her friend's house short and returned to her own house.

She had flown her yoga instructors to Miami to unwind and meditate with her friends. ("I have yoga with me wherever I go," she explained.) Gwyneth, on the other hand, was uninterested in yoga at the moment and spent the remainder of the day moping at Madonna's.

Gwyneth spent the entire night on her cell phone, much to Madonna's chagrin, talking to Ben Affleck, who was in Boston. "You are absolutely smothering that poor man," Madonna was overheard telling Gwyneth. Please disconnect the phone and enjoy the evening."

"Oh, but I miss my sweet little Benny," Gwyneth sobbed. A witness said Madonna rolled her eyes. "Your sweet little Benny is going to jump ship if you don't stop acting so needy," she went on to say. Madonna stepped away from the willowy Gwyneth, who was sitting on the floor embracing her knees.

There was much speculation as to why Madonna was so irritated by Jennifer Lopez's appearance. The fact was that she was enraged by statements made by the singer about her and Gwyneth in a recently released interview.

Lopez said of Madonna, "Do I believe she's a fantastic performer? Yeah. Is she a fantastic actor in my opinion? No. My profession is acting. 'Hey, don't spit on my craft,' I say. "I don't remember anything she was in," she said of Gwyneth. Some folks become overheated by association. "I knew more about her and Brad Pitt than I did about her work." Madonna also learnt from mutual acquaintances that Lopez had made other disparaging remarks about her that were not included in the released interview.

"Let's go dancing," Madonna finally said. Then she and her entourage went to Bar Room, one of the nightclubs run by Ingrid (who is now also a talent manager for Victor Calderone, a DJ who remixes many of Madonna's songs). Within fifteen minutes, Madonna was encircled by a throng of enthusiastic people, each begging for a single, precious second of her attention. Every time Marilyn Monroe entered a room, George Cukor noted, "it was an occasion." The same could be said about Madonna. She moved slowly and methodically through the enthusiastic crowd, smiling and greeting everyone as if the gathering were in her honour. She was quickly engulfed by a crowd of revellers.

Meanwhile, Guy Ritchie sat alone in the bar.

Guy would comment that it never failed to amaze him how he became nearly invisible whenever he was with Madonna in public. Most people ignored him in order to focus their attention on his internationally recognized girlfriend and whatever she was doing and with whom she was doing it.

"Guy, get over here," Madonna yelled from the crowd. "I want you to meet someone."

Guy Ritchie, looking tired, turned to a man he didn't realise was a reporter for a Miami daily. Before taking a sip, he lifted his glass to him. He then stood up. "Hopefully, next New Year's Eve," he said, his voice tired and flat, "I will be home, in bed."

The New Year's Eve party was in full flow by four a.m. Madonna got up on a table and began dancing furiously to the rhythm as the hypnotic strains of pumping techno music filled the room. "C'mon up here," she teased Gwyneth Paltrow.

Gwyneth jumped upon the table to join her companion after a brief pause. Madonna and Gwyneth locked eyes and began dancing, both obviously in a sexual trance, their moves brazenly sensuous, much to the delight of partygoers. They teased and beckoned each other as they performed what appeared to be an impromptu version of the tsamikos (a Greek ritualistic dance in which each dancer clutches the corner of a white handkerchief held aloft — except there was no handkerchief between the two friends).

Even though the music was already loud, it seemed to get louder.

One can only speculate on the pictures that may have crossed Madonna's mind as she danced unrestrainedly. It was the millennium's end. She had been thinking about Lourdes ever since she was born. Faces from the past may have flashed before her while blinded by streams of colour from dazzling lights — snapshots of Christopher Flynn and Camille Barbone and Dan Gilroy and Erica Bell and Jellybean Benitez and Sean Penn and Warren Beatty and John Kennedy, Jr., and Sandra Bernhard and Carlos Leon and Andy Bird and all the rest — names and faces of friends and foes from years gone by, all charging forward in a nostalgic rush of millennial reflectiveness,

While Gwyneth Paltrow strolled around the table, Madonna circled her like a hunter inspecting her delectable prey. Madonna gazed at Gwyneth with ravenous eyes, just as she had always weighed up her career, each challenge perceived as an adversary compelled to bend to her control. Madonna pounced, as if she couldn't hide her desire for warm young flesh any longer. She grasped Gwyneth and pushed her back, arching her spine. Gwyneth gave in when she was forced to do so by her friend's will. Then, while the audience applauded and whistled in agreement, Madonna did what she does best: she defied expectations. She kissed Gwyneth on the lips, letting herself go, surrendering to Gwyneth Paltrow, surrendering to the moment, breathing life into it and then living it for all it was worth.

Gwyneth continued to move her body to the music, her face stunning in its focus as she returned the kiss, joyously immersed in Madonna's Moment. Gwyneth stayed in motion on the table when Madonna eventually let her go, now with a delighted smile and never looking more alive, more lovely. As they witnessed Gwyneth become one with the thumping, booming music, onlookers continued to applaud and stomp in time. Her romantic difficulties, her fears about this guy or that guy, seemed to have been obliterated, utterly erased, by Madonna's Moment.

Madonna jumped off the table to see Gwyneth Paltrow, the sweet and innocent and naive prototype of the new generation of blonde, seductive celebrity, dance on a tabletop – after being kissed by another woman. Who knows what Gwyneth was thinking, or how the experience would affect her life, if at all. However, for Madonna, it was just another example of her habitual disrespect for others. If anything, it had been a kiss that highlighted her personality's beautiful permanence. Yes, she has evolved. Yes, she has softened. But, Kabbalah or no Kabbalah, she's still the same woman she's always been: a woman at her best when she creates outrageous moments and then completely immerses herself in them, pushing everyone else to participate, whether they like it or not.

Madonna nodded in appreciation, her eyes sparkling, as Gwyneth Paltrow continued her one-woman act on the tabletop, lost in her own joy. Then she yelled, raising her voice above the clamour and doing her best Austin Powers impression. "Yeah, baby," Madonna exclaimed to her pal. "Yeah, baby!"

32. Music

Madonna has been a confirmed, card-carrying icon for nearly two decades by the year 2000. She'd done it all in the world of pop stardom. She appeared out of nowhere — not on the back of a celebrity mentor or as a protégée of any famous person — to release a single record that quickly blossomed into a repertoire of international, multi million-selling singles.

She'd done concert tours all around the world, establishing herself as a compelling performer in the process. She'd grown into an accomplished songwriter and record producer. She has appeared in films and on Broadway. She founded businesses, producing millions of dollars for herself, her entertainment empires, and the people around her. She did make a sort of comeback with the Grammy Award-winning Ray of Light. By the turn of the century, it would appear that Madonna the pop diva had accomplished everything as one of the most controversial as well as most emulated female performers in show business history. After establishing herself in practically every category she attempted, a self-respecting pop singer had only one task left: release another hit album.

Maintaining pop popularity is just as difficult as achieving it, as every million-selling artist will confirm. Michael Jackson, the only other pop singer in show business as commercially and artistically successful as Madonna, had seen his career decline substantially by the late twentieth century. Of course, like Madonna, Jackson's legacy as one of the greatest entertainers of all time would be secure even if he never recorded another single or stepped onto another stage. Nonetheless, his inability to keep up with the ever-changing, trend-driven world of pop music became glaringly apparent in the late 1990s with the release of HIStory: Past, Present, and Future, Book I, a two-disc anthology comprising previously released and new songs. Even a frenzied, supercharged duet between the King of Pop and his sister Janet dubbed "Scream" couldn't save the CD's sales. Madonna's peers, Prince and Janet, had also seen their record sales decline in recent years, with both superstars' CD sales far below what they were in their salad days.

By the late 1990s and early 2000, Madonna, the aforementioned artists, the music industry as a whole, and indeed the entire contemporary pop music world, had been taken over by what will most likely be a fleeting trend for "boy bands" and sexy, teenage female bubble-gum artists, with the million-selling Backstreet Boys, N'Sync, Britney Spears, and Christina Aguilera leading the charge. Still, Madonna's career was far from stagnant at the start of the new year. Ray of Light had sold millions of copies globally, and the project had been praised for being daring and refreshing. However, some of Madonna's detractors saw Light as just another premeditated ploy on the artist's side to capitalise on rave-inspired electronica music, which was mostly off popular pop's radar until Madonna got her hands on it.

Detractors failed to recognize that Ray of Light reflected Madonna's particular interests at the time; she wasn't simply exploiting a new sound; it was one she had studied and appreciated. Being a mature pop singer with a diverse professional background hasn't dampened her hunger for daring new music. While she still enjoys listening to songs from classic Hollywood musicals like "Singin' in the Rain" in the privacy of her home and office, Madonna also enjoys the work of alternative artists and eclectic musicians who are virtually unknown to the general public, such as Anoushka Shankar, daughter of Indian music legend Ravi Shankar.

Madonna came across an album tape from writer/producer Mirwais Ahmadzai, who had previously praised her musical abilities, while listening to the various demo tapes and other music that poured into the Maverick Records offices on a daily basis from both aspiring and established songwriters and producers. Except for rave music fans,

Mirwais (he rarely uses his last name) is almost unknown to American pop music fans. "I heard it and thought, 'This is the sound of the future.'" 'I have to meet this person,' Madonna told Rolling Stone. "So I did, and we got along great." And the same thing happened to [Ray of Light producer] William Orbit."

Madonna and Mirwais developed such a chemistry in a hurriedly arranged meeting that Madonna determined that the "sound of the future" would also be the sound of her forthcoming album. She and the producer were in the studio three weeks after shaking hands; the majority of the music was recorded in London beginning in September 1999. The record was nearly finished by the end of January 2000.

Madonna has always believed that competition among her producers is the greatest way to get the most out of them, although William Orbit indicated he didn't mind Mirwais being present. In any case, neither producer would learn the outcome of the other's efforts until the album's lengthy mastering process in London.

Because William Orbit was already aware of Madonna's eccentricities in the studio, it was up to Mirwais to become acquainted with the artist's creative working approach. The Frenchman, who was as much a technician as a musician, would continually fiddle with the music tracks, adding effects and subtracting others, overlaying some sounds and remixing others. Madonna, like many artists with a clear idea of what they want in the studio, is impatient, and Mirwais's plodding style would frequently drive her to distraction. "I just put my foot down and said, 'It's good enough now,'" she remembered. We've finished. We've finished working on it.' He [Mirwais] could just sit in front of his computer screen, modifying, refining, editing, cutting, pasting — whatever he wanted. And it would never come to an end. But life is too short for such nonsense. In the studio, my persona is 'I'm in a rush.' I think he was turned off by the fact that I understood exactly what I wanted and wasn't interested in a lot of extraneous details in the production."

"She took a big risk with someone like me," Mirwais told a reporter after finishing the record. "Once you reach that level of celebrity, you can just work in the mainstream and stay there." Everything she undertakes is a challenge for her, and I admire this type of attitude."

When the work was finished, which took place in London, Los Angeles, and New York, the result was Music, a slick, odourless world of pop melodies and swirling electronic pop funk in which Madonna's subtle, often apathetic feeling is often the only living thing on the terrain. Music, despite its superb gadgetry, is nothing if not passionate. "Impressive Instant," rife with abstract sounds and driving grooves designed to do exactly what the synthesised refrain suggests, put the listener in a trance, and "Amazing," a stylized, guitar-powered, uptempo Orbit collaboration that could have been the musical cousin to "Beautiful Stranger" (the song Madonna and Orbit contributed to the Austin Powers: The Spy Who Shagged Me soundtrack). "I Deserve It," a gloomy, acoustic guitar ballad clearly dedicated to Guy Ritchie ("This Guy was made for me," Madonna says), would also be featured.

Of course, the project's centrepiece would be its first single and title track, "Music." The song is a blast of electronic funk-pop, a dance anthem that pushes into the future while also conjuring up pictures and feelings for the good ol' days of disco (with its affectionate cry out to "Mr. DJ," a relic of disco's past). It's a sparse, deliberate arrangement that quickly grows on you.

The entertaining video, like the song's lyrics, would have a very simple storyline that would go no further than three females out on the town searching for fun. The idea was inspired by the late 1970s and early 1980s, when young Madonna Ciccone and her friends Debi Mazar and Nikki Harris would prowl Manhattan's varied club and art scene in pursuit of music and romance. Initially, actresses were cast as Madonna's video entourage. However, when the women proved to be too gorgeous and stiff, a dissatisfied Madonna called Mazar and Haris in the middle of the shoot and asked them to join her on set.

Madonna would shamelessly imitate the notion of "Ghetto Fabulous" — an over-the-top look popularised by East Coast rap and urban music stars like Sean "Puffy" Combs, Lil' Kim, and Mary J. Blige and characterised by designer clothes and floor-length furs, gaudily accessorised with gold and diamonds (including in the teeth) — for the video, just as she plugged into the electronica scene for the music. Puffy is serious when he steps out of his Bentley dressed like this. However, in the "Music" video, Madonna would wear her flash and gold with a flirtatious wink. The video's eccentric limousine driver was played by British comedian Ali G, whose bold, irreverent tendencies thrill Madonna whenever she visits England. (In character, Ali G conducted a television chat show, attacking politicians and other upstanding members of the British public sector.)

Madonna had high aspirations for Music at the end of January 2000. "I have to stay current," she said during lunch with two friends in Los Angeles, where some of the tunes were being completed. In a chocolate brown Balenciaga jacket and Donna Karan jeans, she looked stunning. Even though her hair was pushed up and she was wearing enormous sunglasses, she garnered a lot of attention. "God help me," she added while being served a tomato and mozzarella salad, "but I guess I'll have to share radio air time with Britney Spears and Christina Aguilera." She sighed and shrugged her shoulders. "What choice do I have?"

"Well, you could always retire," one of her pals jokingly said.

Madonna used a napkin to dab at her lips. "But what would the music business be like without me?" she joked.

33. Happy Endings

Perhaps no one is more proud of Madonna's accomplishments than her father, Tony Ciccone. While he did not support her aim of becoming a dancer and had hoped she would attend college first, he fully understood her desire to "make something of herself, which she did — boy, did she ever!"

When Rocco was born ill and early, Tony proposed to his daughter, over the phone from his vineyard in northern Michigan, that she summon a priest to perform the final rites. Though Madonna is dubious about such ceremonies, it's a measure of her love for her traditional Italian-American father that she even considered giving Rocco final rites. As it turned out, such a sacrament was unnecessary. When it was confirmed that the baby would be healthy, Tony and his wife, Joan, sobbed into one other's arms — and then toasted the new addition to the family, Tony's eighth grandchild, with a nice wine. "Sometimes I think I'm better as a grandfather than I probably was as a father," he admits at this point. "But, let's face it, Madonna was a special case," he said. "I think anyone would sympathise with the father who had the job of raising Madonna."

Tony Ciccone began his hard work on the structure of the Ciccone Vineyards and Winery the day after Rocco's birth, a vineyard that would open to the public a month later on a hilltop between the Grand Traverse Bay tourist town of Sutton Bay and the hills of the Leelanau Peninsula. Tony established his vineyard after retiring from his career as a physicist and engineer at General Dynamics in Detroit in 1994. It is dedicated to his parents, Gaetano and Michelina, who came to the United States three years before he was born from Pacentro, Italy. The Ciccone Vineyards has been a joint initiative for Tony and his wife, Joan, Madonna's stepmother, with whom she never got along as a child but with whom she is now fairly close thirty-three years later.

"It's our life together," he says proudly of his winery, one of twenty-five in Michigan, "mine and my wife's." Plantings include Pinot Grigio, Dolcetto, Cabernet Franc, and Chardonnay. "I think it keeps Joan and me close, even at our age," he adds of the winery. "We raised vegetables in Rochester [Michigan] before owning the winery," he goes on to say. "My father was also a vegetable farmer." Excellent work. The Ciccones have always been reliable employees."

Tony explains that he began producing grapes about five years ago. Joan bought him an antique grape press as a surprise. "He'd always wanted to own a winery," she says. "It was his fantasy. We knew it would be difficult. But when the Sutton Bay property came on the market, we knew we had to get it." (The Ciccones will not say whether Madonna helped pay for the fifteen-acre property.)

Most of his neighbours have no idea Madonna is Tony's daughter. "I don't advertise it," he explains. "It's not required. They'll find out if they don't. I never tell them. Some people are aware. However, they make no fuss about it."

As an adult and a mom, Madonna seemed to recognize that Tony was doing his absolute best when he was raising her, and that his marriage to Joan was not a betrayal of his first wife, but his only option if he was to move on with his life — and provide his children a mother.

Nothing, without a doubt, develops a person more than being a parent. Madonna appeared to be identifying with the parent position rather than the kid role, putting her on the other side of the table for the first time. Perhaps she realised she needed her father more than she needed her anger, and so she was finally able to let go of part of it. Indeed, seeing things through the eyes of a parent was a good omen for Madonna, as it would allow for big adjustments in her relationship with her father.

"I love my father," she says today. "He's the type of guy who says what he means and means what he says." I'm in the same boat. Anyone who knows me knows that I am, at least in that way, my father. He, like myself, is strict. I hope you enjoy my love. His work ethic has been instilled in me. Now that I have a family, I have so much respect for him and the way he attempted to keep our family together while I was a spoiled brat. He didn't have the same privileges I did. It's difficult to see all of that before having children."

Some of Madonna's siblings have fared less well in life than she has, perhaps emphasising the contrast in her personality and determination to meet the obstacles of her surroundings. She has blamed the Ciccone children's instability on her mother's death. "I come from a vast family of emotional cripples in various forms. We're all quite emotionally needy due to my mother." Whereas some of her siblings may have let the trauma of their mother's death to damage their futures, Madonna managed to channel hers into something positive.

Madonna's closest friend is her younger brother Christopher, who accompanied her on several musical tours before opening his own restaurant. Despite some resentment after she discussed his homosexuality with a gay magazine without his consent in 1991, Christopher is her most devoted sibling. Since then, Christopher has travelled alongside his sister, serving as artistic director on her performance tours. (Because of his influential position in the organisation, many in her employ referred to him as "the Pope.") He also designed the interiors of some of her residences. "She has her own vision," he says. "I present her with a fresh perspective. Others do as well. But it's not the case with us. We fight a lot, and either she or I win, but we never give up. We're both not afraid to be direct, and Madonna always knows what she wants."

In addition to owning the restaurant Orient in New York, he also has a stake in the popular restaurant Atlantic in Los Angeles, which

Madonna frequents. "Our father spent the majority of his time preparing us for the rest of our lives," he explains. He taught me the value of honesty, loyalty, and the truth. He instilled in us the value of self-control. Every day, we went to church. He was responsible for our sense of art, drama, and decadence."

While Madonna has a close relationship with Christopher, she is separated from her other two brothers. Martin is a recovering alcoholic who has had a lot of ups and downs in his life and profession. He has worked as a disc jockey and a building contractor in the Detroit region. Martin suffered a well-publicised setback in his treatment barely a day after being discharged from a rehabilitation clinic (paid for by his famous sister) in the early 1990s, during Madonna's "Blonde Ambition" tour. Perhaps unfairly, he appears in his sister's Truth or Dare video to be incoherent and irresponsible, and either too drunk or too bewildered to attend her show and visit her afterwards. The events are structured in such a way that Madonna feels let down by his actions, making her the victim, rather than the more sympathetic thought that the unhappy, intensely scrutinised Martin may be a victim of Madonna's popularity. Madonna lost patience with Martin after his third DUI arrest and a judge's threat to jail him. In 1994, he told a journalist in the United States, "Madonna won't lift a finger to help me." Since then, the two have not been very close. "This is not the sister I grew up with, who mothered me, who was so full of compassion," he tells me. "I guess fame really changes people." (Martin was a patient at the Chabad Rehabilitation Center in Los Angeles in December 2000, being treated for an addiction.)

Madonna has responded to Martin, saying, "He's very tortured." I had to break him of the habit of calling me whenever he needed help. Martin must love me for who I am, not for how much money I have."

Mario, her half-brother, is a former cocaine addict with a history of troubles. He was facing a ten-year prison sentence on a burglary conviction at one time. Only until Madonna engaged a high-powered legal team to defend him on charges that he had broken into a florist's in Rochester, Michigan, and absconded with approximately $2,000 did he find salvation. He was on parole with a three-month suspended jail sentence for allegedly beating his then-girlfriend at the time. It was his third conviction in six months, following charges of battering a motorist and breaking a police officer's nose. "My big sister can't tame me," he has stated. "She has no right to lecture me because I am who I am." "I'm not even a fan of her music."

Anthony and Paula, Madonna's other siblings, are both television producers, and Melanie is a musician's manager in Los Angeles. Madonna's half-siblings, Jennifer and Mario, have a friendly but distant relationship with her.

"We've had a hard time, but the family tries to stay strong," Tony stated. "They mature." They are in charge of their own lives. "I'm in charge of mine. "Tony reverts to the affectionate diminutive of his daughter's childhood. "So maybe I wasn't the greatest father in the world, but life wasn't easy for any of us." He claims he has never felt compelled to respond to anything Madonna or his other children have said about him. "Because we're Italians." We know deep down that we love each other. That is the only thing that matters. You can't always be nearby. But life is short, and there is always tomorrow.

"But, Madonna and I have been closer than people know," he says at the end. "She's more at ease now that she has Lourdes and Rocco to look after." "Look at how much things have changed for her," he exclaims. "This is how a book would end if you were writing one." It would end happily. "Everyone appreciates a happy ending..."